CONCERN
for Education

CONCERN
for Education

ESSAYS ON CHRISTIAN
HIGHER EDUCATION
1958–1966

edited by **Virgil Vogt**

with a Foreword by
Michael G. Cartwright

CASCADE *Books* • Eugene, Oregon

CONCERN FOR EDUCATION
Essays on Christian Higher Education, 1958–1966

Copyright © 2010 Wipf and Stock Publishers. All rights reserved. Except for brief quotations in critical publications or reviews, no part of this book may be reproduced in any manner without prior written permission from the publisher. Write: Permissions, Wipf and Stock Publishers, 199 W. 8th Ave., Suite 3, Eugene, OR 97401.

Cascade Books
An Imprint of Wipf and Stock Publishers
199 W. 8th Ave., Suite 3
Eugene, OR 97401

www.wipfandstock.com

ISBN 13: 978-1-55635-988-0

Cataloging-in-Publication:

CONCERN for education : essays on Christian higher education, 1958–1966 / edited by Virgil Vogt ; foreword by Michael G. Cartwright.

xiv + 152 p. ; 23 cm.

ISBN 13: 978-1-55635-988-0

1. Anabaptists—History—20th century. 2. Anabaptists—theology. I. Vogt, Virgil, 1934–. II. Cartwright, Michael G. III. Yoder, John Howard. IV. Title.

BX8116 .C66 2010

Manufactured in the U.S.A.

Contents

Editor's Note • vi

Foreword by Michael G. Cartwright • vii

PART I: Articles by John Howard Yoder

1 Christian Education: Doctrinal Orientation • 3

2 A Syllabus of Issues Facing the Church College • 21

3 Theological Statements for a Philosophy of Mennonite Education • 49
 Co-authored with Paul M. Lederach

PART II: Articles from *CONCERN* 13

4 Church and Mennonite College • 67
 Albert J. Meyer and Walter Klaassen

5 The Bethel Experience in Retrospect • 108
 Joanne Zerger Janzen

6 Christian Life at Conrad Grebel College • 112
 Walter Klassen

7 The Bluffton College Christian Fellowship • 127
 Henry Rempel

8 Christian Communal Living on the Tabor Campus • 134
 Steve Behrends

9 Tabor College Christian Fellowship Association • 136

10 The Church on Eastern Mennonite College • 139
 Glenn M. Lehman

11 The Church on Campus, Present and Future: What Are the Issues? • 143
 Harold E. Bauman

Afterword by Virgil Vogt • 151

Editor's Note

The first two articles in Part 1 by John Howard Yoder, written respectively in 1958 and 1964, were unpublished documents from the Yoder Papers in the Mennonite Archives at Goshen College. The third article was originally prepared by John Howard Yoder and Paul Lederach as part of a committee charged with the responsibility to articulate a philosophy of education for the Mennonite Church. It was published as an appendix to the book *Mennonite Education: A Philosophy of Education for the Mennonite Church* by Daniel Hertzler (Herald Press, 1971). The articles in Part 2 of this book were first printed in the *Concern* pamphlet 13 in 1966 under the editorship of Virgil Vogt. For a fuller background to the *Concern* publications, read the front pieces to *The Roots of CONCERN* (Eugene, OR: Cascade, 2009). What now follows was printed at the beginning of *Concern* 13:

> *Concern* is an independent pamphlet series dealing with questions of Christian renewal. The sponsoring group shares general responsibility for editing and publishing, but since articles are published for the purpose of discussion, they do not purport to be definitive nor does the sponsoring group necessarily concur in the views expressed.

Foreword

As an administrator of a United Methodist affiliated university, I know that Christian colleges and universities of all kinds confront a host of problems and opportunities in the first decade of the twenty-first century. The problems range from the escalating cost of tuition and increased burdens of deferred maintenance to the nagging questions about how to approach the tasks of faculty development for mission and the recruitment of students in a world of growing diversity. Challenges include the pressure to "deliver" courses on various kinds of "platforms" while demonstrating that the learning goals of the courses that they offer are actually being achieved as displayed in measurable data about the various indicators of outcomes that they track from year to year in order to assure a dubious public that the education that is offered is worth the cost.

These are but a few of the factors that contribute to the commodification of higher education, a phenomenon that is made all the more difficult to withstand given that institutions find themselves competing with one another in what some analysts have called the "experience economy."[1] Paradoxically, students seek out opportunities in the marketplace of higher education for the kinds of meaningful educational experiences in which they are likely to find themselves transformed while enrolled at colleges or universities that claim to "change lives" in some sense or another. Meanwhile, at least some church-related colleges and universities still attempt to engage such consumer-driven desires in ways that keep alive the possibility that students will learn how *not* to be "conformed to this world, but be transformed by the renewal of their minds" (Rom 12:1–2) as St. Paul stated. To say that the situation of Christian

---

1. B. Joseph Pine II and James H. Gilmore, *The Experience Economy: Work is Theatre and Every Business a Stage* (Boston: Harvard Business School Press, 1999).

higher education is unstable in the twenty-first century is probably to understate what most faculty and administrators at church-related colleges experience from day to day, but no one can afford to ignore the ongoing challenge to imagine what it might mean to carry out the project of the what Michael Budde and John Wright have described as "the ecclesially-based university."[2]

With all the contemporary ferment in church-related higher education in view, the publication of this set of essays by scholars and church leaders associated with the *Concern* group is a welcome contribution. To look back at these materials is to be reminded that even before most colleges and universities experienced the full effects of the disestablishment of American Protestantism, Mennonite church leaders and scholars were thinking through the questions associated with living in a *post-Christendom* world. We should not expect to find a consensus about what it meant to offer a non-Christendom oriented form of church-related higher education so much as a vigorous debate about what integrity means whenever a particular church body attempts to make a particular project of higher education possible. What we *can* expect to find—and indeed, I think, we do find in these reports from Mennonite educators—is a fascinating set of descriptions of the experiments of the faculty and students who attempted to embody the Anabaptist vision in particular places in the mid-1960s.

With this in mind, I predict that readers of this second collection of *Concern* essays will make three kinds of discoveries.

First, whether or not readers are already familiar with the *Concern* group,[3] they will be interested to learn that there was such a searching conversation about the direction of Mennonite higher education in the 1950s and 1960s. The quest for a more radical expression of Christian witness that is not defined by the pretensions of Christendom is a common aspiration in these texts. The authors of the articles published in the thirteenth issue of *Concern* (1966) did not always agree about how to proceed, but they did not want the church's mission in higher education to be defined by the state. In retrospect, some observers would argue that one of the effects of such conversations is to foster

2. Michael L. Budde and John Wright, eds., *Conflicting Allegiances: The Church-Based University in a Liberal Democratic Society* (Grand Rapids: Brazos, 2003).

3. See Virgil Vogt's "Foreword" to *The Roots of CONCERN: Writings on Anabaptist Renewal*, ed. Virgil Vogt (Eugene, OR: Cascade, 2009) vii–ix.

the development of a "new Christendom."⁴ Make no mistake about it, though, the future of Christian learning that these writers envisioned was counter-cultural when compared with so-called mainline Protestant institutions of higher education of that same era.

Second, I suspect that some readers will be intrigued to learn about the various institutions of higher education associated with the Mennonite tradition of Christianity precisely because the story of Mennonite higher education has not been told in a synoptic way that could distinguish such institutions from Quaker and Church of the Brethren colleges. Even in the twenty-first century, there is a tendency to lump the historic peace churches together. The essays about the institutions that today we know as Bluffton University, Goshen College, and Bethel College display different approaches to education for Christian discipleship. However, there is more than a family resemblance in the missions and identity of these church colleges during the mid-twentieth century. I also think there is much to be learned from the intra-Mennonite conversations about voluntariness of student participation, and their struggles to engage the Niebuhrian rhetoric of responsibility and freedom associated with Christian realism while holding to their commitment to non-violence, which they also commended to the students on their campuses.

While the topics of these conversations may sound familiar to twenty-first-century Christian educators in colleges and universities, more often than not the character and scale of institutional practices may not be. For example, I suspect that most American readers are still unfamiliar with Conrad Grebel College, the institution that was created by Mennonites to operate independently of—but cooperate in some areas with—the University of Waterloo in Ontario. Once they have read Walter Klaassen's account of the story of what happened in the early years of that institution, however, I predict that they will want to find out more about the history of this institution named for one of the first Anabaptist martyrs. Among other things, they will see how the faculty and staff at that fledgling institution were attempting to live out

---

4. Mark A. Noll and James Turner, *The Future of Christian Learning: An Evangelical and Catholic in Dialogue*, ed. Thomas Albert Howard (Grand Rapids: Brazos, 2008). In his essay, "Reconsidering Christendom" (31–43), Noll argues that this has been the case.

what it means to be church and academy with appropriate attention to the purposes of each.

The discussion of issues facing Mennonite colleges in the 1960s that Albert J. Meyer and Walter Klaassen offered in their overview is also illuminating. The fact that this article begins with a discussion of five important Christian practices may also fascinate those who are more familiar with the *Practice Our Faith* series edited by Dorothy Bass. Mennonite educators were wrestling with a host of questions about the appropriate relationship of *academe* and *ekklesia*, while also keeping in mind the freedom that is appropriate to each. As one reads these essays, it is clear that lessons drawn from the experience of Bethel and Goshen were shared with the faculty at Conrad Grebel and vice versa. In addition, the fact that leaders such as Albert Meyer would subsequently exercise leadership in the Mennonite Board of Education for more than three decades ensured that at least some of the fruits of these conversations were institutionalized, and that what each institution learned in the process was disseminated to the others.

I anticipate that readers will also make a third set of discoveries when they take the measure of John Howard Yoder's individual contributions to these conversations about higher education. On the one hand, Yoder played the role of "the devil's advocate" by preparing "a syllabus of issues" that Mennonite "church colleges" were confronting in the mid-twentieth century. In that piece we see the kind of tough-minded analysis about stewardship of resources, including the kind of financial parsimony, that is appropriate to a church that is "missionary minded." Yoder also provides a fascinating analysis of issues surrounding the conjunction of "Christian education" and "liberal arts" education that turns on different notions of "utility." Yoder chides those who would want to shun questions of usefulness even while he probes what Christians mean when they talk about notions of "higher uses" of education. On the other hand, we learn more about Yoder's own views about the possibilities and limits of the education and formation of the people of God in the essay on "Christian Education." For those scholars who are interested in questions of Christian formation and/or spiritual formation, these essays provide some of the most explicit claims that Yoder ever made about the education of children and adults.

Some readers may wonder why these pieces by Yoder have never been published before. There are at least two reasons—the first contingent and the second circumstantial. Yoder had been asked to write the piece on "Christian Education" for an earlier issue of *Concern*. During the 1958–59 academic year, Yoder wrote his paper but the responses that were commissioned never materialized. Once the occasions for which these texts were prepared had passed, he set them aside thinking at the time that non-Mennonites would not be interested in a conversation that was primarily "in-group" in character. Thereafter, as Yoder recalled, "the question died down when it became obvious that for purely quantitative reasons church-governed high school education would remain a minority privilege whether we liked it or not."[5] We are fortunate that these materials are available to shed light on Yoder's views about Christian higher education during this early period of his life and work.

Finally, I believe that the publication of these materials presents new opportunities for engagement with the theological challenges and educational opportunities of our own time and place. I can imagine at least two ways that *Concern for Education* will be used. First, the forthcoming publication of Gerald Schlabach's book *Unlearning Protestantism* by Brazos Press[6] already presents the prospect for twenty-first-century engagement with the two papers written by John Howard Yoder as well as raises important questions about the instability of the *post-Christendom* vision of radical Christianity to which various other Concern group authors aspired. And as Yoder's work continues to evoke responses from the wider ecumenical community (including Orthodox as well as Catholics and Protestants), questions about the ecclesiology that informed the *Concern* group's conception of higher education will need to be probed further, and these essays provide a very helpful place to dig in to that nest of issues.

Beyond the value of these documents for thinking through questions about the role of the church in carrying out God's mission of reconciliation in the world, there is yet another use that I think these materials can be put in the years to come. And that is to help bring focus to the renewed conversation about what it means to be "called" to Christian discipleship. The emergence of a network of eighty-eight

---

5. Letter from John Howard Yoder to Dennis Stoltzfus, July 19, 1991, in the Papers of John Howard Yoder, Archives of Associated Mennonite Biblical Seminary.

6. See Gerald W. Schlabach, *Unlearning Protestantism: Sustaining Christian Community in an Unstable Age* (Grand Rapids: Brazos, 2010).

institutions of higher education (initially funded by the Religion Division of Lilly Endowment, Inc.) in the USA that are committed to offering curricular and co-curricular opportunities for theological exploration of vocation suggests a second prospect for engagement that I think is likely to occur in the years to come. Those faculty and administrators who are part of this broader set of efforts to cultivate conversations about Christian formation on the campuses of church-related colleges and universities would be advised to take a glance at the conversations in Mennonite Colleges in the 1960s, not least because of the fact that we will see that some contemporary experiments that we are attempting to carry out may not be as innovative as we would like to think. And more than forty years before anyone thought about the intentional communities associated with the "new monasticism," Mennonite educators were developing covenants that ordered their life together around practices of Christian discipleship.

I am taking the time and space to remind readers about these predecessor efforts because we are not the first generation of Christian educators that has struggled with the need to re-engage the parent denominations that founded the colleges and universities where we teach and learn alongside students. Many faculty and administrators in church-related institutions have benefited from the efforts of the Coalition of Christian Colleges and Universities (CCCU) and the Lilly Fellows Program (LFP) network of church-related colleges and universities to promote coherence in the mission and identity of church-related higher education over the past quarter of a century. This collection of essays should serve as a reminder that the conversations of the Concern group were already pointing to the need for greater clarity about the relationship of *ekklesia* to *academe*. And of course, that is still one of the most significant challenges and opportunities that we face in the twenty-first century.

In the wake of the Concern conversation, John Howard Yoder made contributions to a series of workshops and conferences organized by the Mennonite Board of Education. The 1964 "Workshop on the Church College" provided the opportunity to begin conversations that included all of the colleges related to the Mennonite Church (but not the institutions of the General Conference Mennonite body). The papers by Yoder, Krauss, and Miller identified critical issues that needed further study and analysis.

Subsequently, a Philosophy of Christian Education Study Committee was formed in response to the emerging recognition (voiced by Albert Meyer as early as 1962) that Mennonites needed to articulate a philosophy of Christian higher education. This group met for the first time in March 1966, at which time they appointed a Philosophy of Christian Education Research Committee that carried out specific tasks that it reported to the study committee over the next four years. The study committee completed its work in 1971. Yoder played an active role on the research committee, particularly with respect to the effort to articulate a theological rationale for Mennonite institutions of higher education.

The results of the study committee's work was published in the spring of 1971 in the book *Mennonite Education: Why and How? A Philosophy of Education for the Mennonite Church* (Scottdale, PA: Herald, 1971) by Daniel Hertzler in collaboration with Don Augsburger, Paul Bender, Ira E. Miller, Laban Peachey, and John Howard Yoder. Paul Lederach and John Howard Yoder prepared the set of theological statements for the Research Committee that were circulated in the spring of 1968 and ultimately published as Appendix A to the aforementioned book. For a chronology of the work of the Study Committee and the Research Committee that carried out the project of producing a theological rationale, see Appendix B in Hertzler et al., 64–66.

Overlapping with this venture but functioning independently was another Lilly Endowment-funded study project to develop a model for theological education in the Free Church tradition sponsored by Associated Mennonite Biblical Seminaries of Elkhart, Indiana. The results of that study were published by Herald Press in 1971 in a volume edited by Ross Bender. As I explained in the editor's introduction to *The Royal Priesthood: Essays Ecumenical and Ecclesiological*, this latter project provided the occasion for Yoder to articulate a "schematic summary of marks of the church" (12–13), which makes explicit central features of Yoder's ecclesiology.

While there are certainly differences between these publications as well as developments in Yoder's own theological thinking, readers will also see a remarkable consistency between the four different documents that were written over a period of ten-to-twelve years. As Gerald Schlabach has argued elsewhere, some members of the Concern group tended to be more anti-institutional than others. Yoder's participation in these efforts displays a different pattern of advocacy of Christian renewal than those who wanted to separate themselves from denominational politics and institution building. That pattern took the form of patient persuasion and careful committee work with fellow church leaders that helped shape an emergent consensus that would inform policies that in turn would be deployed through the Mennonite Board of Education, which was the body that coordinated denomination policy for institutions like Bethel College and Goshen College. In retrospect, we can discern that conceptual connections can be traced back to the conversations initiated by Yoder and others associated with *Concern*.

I have not attempted to compare unpublished versions of these texts with those that were published in the volumes edited by Bender and Yoder to identify what parts are original to John Howard Yoder and which emphases Paul Lederach brought to the text, and I would argue that it would not be helpful to do so. Quite likely, Yoder would not have seen these as occasions for individual display. Rather, as he did on numerous occasions over the course of his lifetime, Yoder was operating as an educator who also held leadership positions in two different Mennonite Church-related institutions—Goshen College and Goshen Biblical Seminary—in the 1960s and 1970s. Whereas the materials that he prepared in the late 1950s were part of an unofficial initiative (of the Concern group) that attempted to prompt wider conversation about the whole range of Christian education ventures, these later efforts were initiated in the context of institutional concerns and denominational questions. When a Lilly Endowment initiative made it possible for Mennonite leaders to think through what were the most appropriate models and/or philosophies of education for colleges and seminaries, Yoder was one of the persons who was called upon to assist with that wider effort. The net result was a set of published documents that display the coherence of Yoder's ecclesiology of Christian peoplehood.

Michael G. Cartwright
Dean of Ecumenical & Interfaith Programs
University of Indianapolis, 2009

PART I

Articles by John Howard Yoder

1

Christian Education
Doctrinal Orientation

John Howard Yoder

The following studies are intended to contribute to current thinking about the management and goals of church-sponsored educational institutions. The two forms in which this problem is especially relevant are firstly the "parochial" school movement which has recently created numerous private elementary and high schools in the U.S. and Canada, and secondly the conception of higher education linked to the simple but meaningful motto, "Culture for Service,"[1] generally understood to mean that a church-supported institution should pioneer in all fields of cultural endeavor.

The questions here raised have their roots primarily in Christian doctrine. At the same time, they spring from the conviction that no ultimate barrier between the doctrinal and the practical is possible, and that therefore both practical arguments and practical proposals belong in a discussion about Christian doctrine in its present meaning. The basis for discussion here submitted makes no claim to any sort of finality nor even to speak for the convictions of all the responsible publishers of

---

1. [The reader should be aware that the phrase "Culture for Service" is the motto of John Howard Yoder's alma mater, Goshen College. —Ed.]

Concern yet it claims to ask questions which must be clearly and biblically answered if current trends in thinking about Christian education are justifiable. The writers and publishers regret that efforts spread over more than a year's time have not succeeded in obtaining for concurrent publication a statement of the position here criticized; such a statement will be welcomed in the future.

The Doctrinal Context of the Problem of Education

The Sociological Formulation of the Problem

Sociologists have worked out with considerable accuracy a description of an historical process that they call the "sect cycle." A religious movement, beginning with an initial period of creative vitality during which it breaks away from surrounding culture, gradually readapts to that same environment with the passing of the generations, with the result that, a few decades or centuries later, it retains only such distinctive features as can be kept at no great cost, such as a peculiar form of worship or a distinctive creed.

There is no doubt of the fact that the Christian church as a whole went through such a "sect cycle." It is not only a movement which repeats itself in Quakerism, Methodism, Campbellism, Adventism, and a host of other movements; the whole of Christendom first of all followed the same oath between the age of the Apostles and that of Augustine. In fact, Christianity followed that oath with greater effectiveness than any other religion, with the possible exception of Islam. Beginning with a group of social "misfits" convinced that this world was not going to be around long and possessed of the absolute necessity of rescuing from its collapse as many individuals as possible, Christianity had become within four centuries the recognized religious expression of Greco-Roman culture, changing what it could of paganism, but also blessing what it could not change, convinced that this world was going to be around a long time and resigned to making the best of it.

The Anabaptists of the sixteenth century, like others before and after them, believed that Christendom, in ceasing to be the primitive church and becoming medieval Europe, had taken the wrong path. They called for a return to the Christianity of the New Testament, and to a very great degree succeeded in reproducing in their day what the church of AD 50 or 80 had been. They believed not only that their church should take this form, but that every true church should do likewise, and that their own church should keep this form. They condemned the "sect cycle" itself.

And yet they could not avoid what they condemned. Sometimes because they were persecuted, and sometimes because they weren't, the Anabaptist and their Amish and Mennonite survivors ceased very soon to be what they had been in the second quarter of the sixteenth century. Some drifted back into the general stream of Western Christendom, retaining little of what had been peculiar to them, apart from a congregational form of organization, a late age of baptism, or a dislike of creedal statements. Others formed their own cultural islands by migration and abandoned the claim to have something that all other Christians should have, as well as the effort to save anyone from the collapse of the world. Differences of both cultural and ethical nature continue to exist, but by and large they have ceased to cost anything.

To the sociologist this is all perfectly normal. It conforms to the pattern. The Christian will, however, ask another question: is it right? Does it conform to God's intention? Is the determinism which makes a "sect" necessarily become a "denomination" (determinism?) to be accepted as a fact which cannot be changed, or is it to be combated as a part of the sin of the world? Here it will serve us to survey the possible answers.

1. One may say that the determinism is itself willed by God. It is good that the primitive church should have become the Roman Catholic church. God uses this process to supplement biblical revelation and to christianize gradually all of civilization. If there be movements of renewal, they must stay within the system; their criticisms may be energetic but they may not be basic challenges to the existence of the system. This is the answer of Catholicism. There may continue to be "sects" (the monastic, mendicant, and teaching orders) that come into life and go through their cycle, but they may never claim that all Christians should take such a path.

2. One may say that medieval Catholicism needed to be corrected at certain points, on certain matters of religious nature, but that the changes should be kept to a minimum. The determinism that the church had followed until about AD 500 can be accepted; a few

abuses introduced later by the papacy can be easily removed. This is the answer of State-Church Protestantism.

3. One may say that medieval Catholicism was right for its time, but that the determinism should continue to evolve, and the church with it. The next stages of that evolution were the Renaissance, rationalism, idealism, evolutionary materialism, and existentialism, and the Christianity that attempts to keep up with this development is modern religious liberalism.

4. One may say that the dissidence of a group like the Anabaptists was right for its time, but that it was also right for their descendants to follow the "sect cycle" and return to a new compromise with culture. Each group which goes through the cycle enriches the total culture somehow, but what really counts is the movement of the total culture and not the separate history of any group; no group can itself be finally right. This would be the view of many Dutch Mennonites and of most American denominations; the sooner a particular group can complete its cycle, the more useful it is, for then it can contribute its peculiar "talent" to the general cultural fund.

5. One may say that the Anabaptists were right, and that their rejection of the "sect cycle" determinism was justified. If this is the case, then the descendants of the Anabaptists also left the right path somewhere; without attempting to place the blame, Christians in our time should seek once again to make of their fellowship a church like that of the New Testament or like that of the Anabaptists or the early Friends or Brethren.

When one attempts to weigh these five positions one against the other, by asking what are, for each, the ultimate criteria of value, one is struck by the fact that the first four basically agree with each other. All four agree that it is hopeless to fight against the determinism that with the passage of time makes any church fit the surrounding culture. All are alike in that there is no clear standard by which the movement of that culture is to be judged. Views 1 and 3 agree that there is no standard at all outside the cultural movement itself and disagree violently only in the choice of which century to consider as ideal. Views 2 and 4 would both hold that scriptural revelation should be authoritative, in some sort of critical function. The present culture should be criticized by the norms of revelation and should try to improve, but the final authority for deciding what Christians and the church should do is not the Bible alone but a reasonable compromise between the Bible and cultural necessity. They see no conceivable point at which the entire church could return to "sect" status within society. Again they differ only in the choice of centuries: view 2 prefers sixteenth-century England, Geneva, or Saxony; view 4 prefers nineteenth-century England or the United States. The choice between these four views can hardly be made on biblical grounds. Most Americans lean to views 3 or 4, out of the same kind of determinism which all four basically accept.

Those who recognize that view 5 is the only one taking biblical authority seriously are faced with a problem which the other views avoid: if we reject the determinism to which all the other views surrender (and the Christian faith in the resurrection is, at bottom, a rejection of all determinisms), how then can we go about rejecting it more effectively? If we know that such grounds have in the past been unsuccessful in transmitting their vision to their children and grandchildren, we are driven to ask whether they could have done otherwise. If they could not have done otherwise, then we must conclude that determinism had the last word whether we accept it or not. We could still decide that it would be good to have a new Anabaptist movement with the formation of a new sect every forty or every four hundred years, but we could no longer really reject the tendency which leads every sect (view 5) to assimilation (view 4).

It would be a serious mistake to think that analysis of the "sect cycle" could really help us to find a true understanding of the church's path in the world. Even if we could trust the sociologists to provide us with infallible guidance, only those who accept positions 1–4 could consistently follow their counsel. We have dealt with this problem, and done so in these terms, only as an introduction to what shall concern us in the problem of church-administered education. For any educational program is the expression of a sociological ideal. Any such program set up by a social group and meant principally for the education of its own young people is by that very fact the expression of a strategy of survival, so that the twin questions must be answered: "What are we trying to save?" and "Are the means we choose appropriate for saving it?" These are the questions the following pages hope to ask, and they must be asked in fully sober recognition of the fact that those groups which in the past sought to escape from the drift toward the mass church and cultural conformity have never succeeded.

The Heritage and Its Transmission

The Christian faith which we are interested in expressing, preserving, propagating, and passing on to our children is not first of all a behavior pattern. We believe, and rightly so, that our Christian life involves a very specific behavior pattern. We believe it involves rejecting some things that are customary in the world around us, and insisting on some things that are not customary or even respected. Yet a strategy of survival for a church or social group, which thinks that this behavior pattern is what needs to be transmitted, and seeks for the most effective ways to transmit it, has already begun with a misjudgment. Our faith involves conscientious objection; yet it is possible to transmit to our young people a behavior pattern involving conscientious objection without having transmitted to them our faith. The possibility of exerting such pedagogical and psychological influences as to reproduce quite faithfully a desired behavior pattern is in fact not an aid to the propagation of true faith, but often a hindrance, for those pedagogical and psychological influences can get in the way of faith.

Nor is the Christian faith which we are interested in expressing, preserving, propagating, and transmitting to our children a set of truths. It is true that God exists and that God created heaven and earth, yet believing and even being able to argue convincingly to that effect is not faith. It is true that all men are sinners and that Jesus Christ, the Son of God, has by His life, death and resurrection, enabled salvation for all who believe; yet even these truths can be accepted, repeated, and passed on to others, without faith. Truth can be defended, exposed, and proved to be true and necessary, without engendering faith.

For the Christian faith that we are interested in expressing, preserving, propagating, and transmitting to our children is a personal relationship of fellowship and obedience with God in Christ through the Spirit. This relationship cannot be established by proofs and defenses, nor can it be ensured by pedagogical and psychological influences. It is the work of a Spirit who blows where He will, and it calls forth a fully personal, fully free, fully individual response in the believer.

The essential truth that was rediscovered for modern times by the Anabaptists of the sixteenth century was just this fact: that if Christian faith is to be true, it must be fully free. A child committed without its consent to the acceptance of Christian behavior patterns or of Christian truths is hindered rather than helped on the path to true faith. He is placed, by infant baptism, in a context where he will have to choose between an independence which will mean rejection of those Christian patterns, and acceptance of the patterns which will mean abandon of his personal integrity.

It is not our present concern to follow, through the spiritual history of the occident, the results of the Reformation having identified birth with entrance into the Christian community. (This has been attempted to some extent in *Concern* No. 1). For our present purpose it suffices to have made the observation that the originality of the Anabaptists was their insistence, founded in their return to the New Testament, that true Christian faith is an adult commitment, involving all of life, made in full awareness of the available alternatives. No one joined their fellowship who was not conscious of a break, which he made final in his baptismal confession, with the world to which he had previously belonged. His confession thus involved first of all the realization that the world is a primary fact of human experience, and that one can be emancipated from it only by the gracious initiative of God.

As long as acceptance of the Anabaptist's faith meant a break with the world and real sacrifice, the pressures of opinion and personal advantage kept alive the real choice between discipleship and conformity to the world. As soon, however, as persecution ceased and prosperity began, the churches of the Anabaptist heritage began to lose that clarity in a new kind of internal worldliness. The totality of the pressures, which play upon the individual's life and choice—livelihood, reputation, influence—began to push people into the church instead of out. The acceptance of the truths and the behavior patterns originally derived from faith became possible without faith and without any costly break with the world. Thus the very forms which had been in earlier generations the sign of nonconformity became a sign of conformity, and the Mennonite communities' success in "holding the young people" through conformity rather than through choice became the source of their spiritual tepidity.

The last century and especially the last half-century have witnessed a far-reaching breakdown of the mechanisms of conformity which had succeeded through three centuries in maintaining an unusual high degree of cultural uniformity. It had been possible during all that time to transmit behavior patterns, with or without faith, since the relatively closed community, the strong family ties, and the lack of communication with other cultures presented the Mennonite young person with no other real choices. To join the church, even when that joining involved the verbal profession of a conscious choice and a break with the world, was really no such thing, for it was the only conceivable way of growing up. For him to refuse the baptism offered him would have required more independence and non-conformity than he was capable of. This situation began to loosen with the improvement in communications and the multiplication of the other paraphernalia of culture; and then really to disintegrate with the coming of generalized public education. The pressures of livelihood, reputation, and influence began once again to push people away from the church, and Mennonite churches began "losing the young people."

(We use the terms "holding" and "losing" as quotations, drawn from general usage; to accept them in our own vocabulary would mean accenting the attitude that we criticize. Both terms assume that the church "has" the young people, in virtue of their birth in Christian homes. The only problem then is to "hold" them. This assumption is only possible for those who baptize their babies. For those who believe that faith is a matter of personal choice, the young people need not to be "held" but to be won.)

Facing this problem, two kinds of strategy were possible. One would have been to accept this new competition from the world as a normal thing, and to profit from its reappearance, in such a way as to state the issue that the Gospel places before every individual, in terms of the call to a clear renunciation of the world. This would have meant not attempting to meet the world on its own level, but facing openly the fact that the normal development of a human being in this fallen world does not lead him into the church. This would have placed the church anew in the basically missionary situation of the early sixteenth century.

The other strategy would have been to attempt to beat the world at its own game. The influences tending to keep young people within the group would, instead of being left to work unconsciously, be taken in hand in a studied way. A conscious effort would be made to prevent acquaintance with thought and types of behavior that deviate from the desired norm. Occupational training that would tend to lead individuals out of their dependence on the group would be avoided. In order to avoid the dangers of unsupervised individual decision, the group would become increasingly precise about its standards, whether in behavior or in thought. Young people would be made to feel that they really had no other choice but to remain in the group and accept baptism at the proper age. The age esteemed to be proper would be brought as low as possible in order to have the young people inside the church where they can be more effectively supervised.

It goes without saying that neither of these strategies has been applied in a pure form in recent church history. In just what propositions the two are mixed, we cannot say. Our only interest is to observe that the more consciously the second type of strategy is used, the more surely the center of attention shifts from the personal and non-manipulable center of Christian faith to its expressions in behavior or thought. This strategy of defense will seek to work against worldly tendencies in dress, in recreation, and in economic life; it will seek to combat unbelief in the interpretation of nature (the evolutionary hypothesis) or of history (nationalism, militarism).

Entirely apart from the question whether such a protective strategy is a human possibility, whether it is feasible in the twentieth century to achieve the necessary degree of educational and psychological control, we must raise the deeper question of principle. Does not the attempt to protect young people from the world in this way render questionable the deep genuineness of their decision, even when it is sincere, to leave the world and follow Christ? Is it not a fact, both in logic and in experience, that a decision made easily in early adolescence when no other really interesting alternatives were available, will seem very questionable to the young person himself when, several years later, he discovers that unbelief in thought and in behavior can be quite respectable sometimes and quite interesting at other times? Some individuals facing this problem struggle through to a reaffirmation of a more mature faith, often with a second decision which in later life will seem to them more important than the first. Others feel cramped but eventually "settle down" to what is expected of them. Still others feel clearly that they were somehow cheated, since the church now asks of them a degree of faithfulness to which they were never aware of having committed themselves. Thus the attempt to take consciously in hand the determinisms acting upon young people results in undermining the genuineness of the very faith it intends to transmit.

It is this writer's conviction, though proofs to the contrary will be welcomed, that if the practice of "holding young people" through the pressures of conformity through three centuries did not preserve spiritual vitality within the churches of the Anabaptist heritage, a more studied and psychologically competent strategy of protection with the same aim is not likely to do much better in the future. We should, therefore, ask ourselves if there is not some means of placing the decision for Christ and the church within a clearer context of choice by permitting the young person to become acquainted with the other claims being made on his loyalty.

This "context of choice" would by no means mean seeking to place the young person in temptation, or deliberately seeking for him an unwholesome environment. But it would mean at least that no studied attempts would be made to create around him and for him an artificially wholesome environment such that when he later meets the world he meets it as a child, having developed no spiritual and intellectual antibodies. Just as a vaccination, by permitting an infection in ideal circumstances, when the body is capable of resistance, is the best protection against a fatal infection at some later time when the resistance is lowered and the germ more virile, so it would seem that the best preparation for meeting life in its full force in the twenties would be to grow gradually into a degree of acquaintance with its sordid fascination in the teens when the support of family and the momentum of childhood training are still strong. It has already happened that entire villages of primitive peoples have succumbed to the common cold, received through their first contact with civilized peoples, for the simple reason that they had never acquired immunity. Isolation is thus completely successful if it can be complete. Within human relations there is no possibility of such isolation, and if Christians sought it they would have forgotten their reason for being in the world.

In practice, this argument would mean that the young person, in that period of life where he becomes aware of his independent personality and begins to seek to relate himself to a broader human environment than that of the family, should normally be permitted to encounter not a selected Christian environment, but the world around him as it is. He should have access, in that encounter, to all the assistance which he can use from family and church, to aid him in interpreting what he finds and in developing his own "antibodies," but this assistance should not be urged on him nor take the form of censorship. The decision for discipleship that he makes in this context of freedom will then be his own. He will know, in essence if not in all its grimy detail, what he is rejecting, and he will have at least some awareness of the absolute claims of what he is accepting. He will not later come to feel that he has been cheated nor to think that the church is asking too much of him.

This point of view is open to attack from two directions. On the optimistic side, there are those who tend to deny that the child of Christian parents should enter the church on the same basis as a former pagan: that is, as a convert. It is their feeling that Christian nurture is an alternative procedure to conversion, which, given good home and church environment, can lead smoothly and without a break from childhood into mature faith.

Now it cannot be denied that there are some kinds of personalities that seem to exemplify this sort of development. Whether they are the majority is highly dubious, but, even if it were, it is eminently dangerous to attempt to base one's view of the nature of the church and of church membership upon what one takes to be normal personality development. The modern American psychologist and religious educator, whose belief is that normal personality development is an unbroken upward line, since the normal personality is basically good, evil being the fault of a situation outside the individual, has come to that conviction not by the study of psychology, but from a theological prejudice. The Christian must question seriously this analysis, not only because it contradicts his own biblically founded knowledge of sin and the world, but also because it is not scientifically honest. It is highly likely that the person who has grown into mature faith without noticeable crisis experience is the person whose "vaccination" began early. Such a child, living in a truly Christian home, but never sheltered artificially from the awareness of sin, could decide, freely, step by step, to reject the world and belong to Christ. This is a kind of conversion. It is a far different thing from the "Christian nurture" which claims to guarantee growth in the right direction by decreasing the awareness of other possibilities.

The other criticism is the basically pessimistic one. It fears that if the young person, especially in adolescence, is permitted to become acquainted with the world and its lures, he is sure to be lost. This prediction is, in all its intended realism, a lack of faith and a surrender to determinism. If the Gospel cannot call people out of the world, it is no Gospel. If what we preach to our young people cannot call them out of the world, then we must ask ourselves if what we are preaching is the Gospel. If placing people in a context of choice where it is possible to choose the wrong is unwise, then God himself made the first mistake when he created Adam and the worst mistake when he let people kill his Son. At the bottom of it all, this pessimism means placing oneself fully on the level of the world. It means agreeing with the world that all human development is determined by physical and psychological necessities; agreeing with the world that Christian faith is a matter of behavior patterns and of truths to be passed on; agreeing with the world that there is no miracle of resurrection, no miracle of faith, no Holy Spirit.

It would thus seem to be the case that the churches of the Anabaptist tradition (and if this be true for the Mennonites, it should be true as well for the Brethren, the Friends, and the Baptists) are called to choose between two possible strategies of survival. On one hand there is the pragmatic strategy which has been functioning through the centuries with quite modest success, but which could be undertaken in a more studied and conscious way. This strategy would seek to control fully all the factors that influence the young person's growth, in order to insure that the desired behavioral and doctrinal patterns be maintained. There is some chance that this strategy might continue to work for some time, and might effectively delay the sect cycle's coming full circle. But it would at the same time be a contradiction in terms. What reason have the churches of the Anabaptist tradition to exist, if they accept the same determinisms and the same identification of the church with human continuity, the same identification of faith and the fruits of faith that the first Anabaptists rejected?

The other choice would be an earnest effort to bring back the church to a missionary context through the radical claim that even the children of Christians need to be won from the world, and that the church's life always depends, not on physical and psychological determinisms, but on the miracle of the Gospel. Whether the church would survive on those terms is something we cannot say, but it might just happen that if such a church really believed that its existence depended on the Holy Spirit rather than on its sociological strategy, the Holy Spirit would come. It might just happen. The New Testament and the Anabaptists thought so, at least that this rejection of all determinisms and survival strategies, launching out into the belief that if the church does not live by miracles she does not live at all, would turn out to be the most effective social strategy, because Jesus Christ is really Lord, and not the principalities and powers, thrones and dominations, determinisms and mechanisms.

If we turn from this general introduction to the question of church-guided education of young people, we observe first of all that the movement toward church primary and secondary schools in the United States has been led by those churches that belong to the medieval state-church tradition. The Roman Catholics, the conservative Calvinists, and the conservative Lutherans lead the movement. These are precisely those churches that are by nature committed to a non-missionary view of the church. They baptize their babies and seek by rigid catechization and strict moral teaching to maintain proper standards of behavior and doctrine. The parochial school is for them an effort to retain, in free America, the cultural monopoly that they had each in its own corner of Europe, in order to survive by use of deterministic forces. There is no reason to hold this against them, for it corresponds to their definition of faith as being primarily doctrinal. For them it is consistent, for they never did accept the biblical and Anabaptist claim that the visible church lives only by evangelization. They are the worldly churches that the Anabaptists left. We must draw at least a warning from the fact that such churches are the leaders in the movement toward parochial schools, for reasons that are consistent with their own understanding of the Christian faith, but not with ours.

There would seem to be three different lines of reasoning tending to favor the parochial schools. The first would be the claim that the state-supported educational system is not competent, and that a private institution can do a better job of providing children and young people with a qualified secular education. Where this argument is relevant, it bears real weight. Such was the case in the time of Christopher

Dock, in the sixteenth-century Moravia and the nineteenth-century Ukraine. Today it might be the case in the American South and in Western Canada. On the primary level it might apply in certain solidly Mennonite communities or on a *Bruderhof*. For the times and places where that argument applies, this present essay brings no challenge. It must however be admitted that this argument does apply to most of the situations in which the organization of parochial schools is being advocated and undertaken. We note firstly, that this argument, though it holds in favor of private schools, does not by any means necessitate that such private schools be church-run. Secondly, it is not generally the case that a parochial school, especially on a high-school level, is technically capable of giving a better education than the existing state schools in most areas of Mennonite population.

The second line of argument, which seems to predominate in the literature which has come to our attention, is that of the mass churches. The church school aims to protect the young people from the world, from ideas and kinds of behavior which might weaken their loyalty to the church. That this view seems to us to be unacceptable, for doctrinal reasons growing from the idea of faith and of the church that it presupposes, has been amply explained.

The third line of argument points to the fact that in many areas of education, a religiously neutral state school is in reality religiously prejudiced and will give to the young person, Christian or not, a factually unbalanced understanding of the world. The young person who faces a deterministic view of history, a Darwinian view of biology, or a materialistic psychology, *may* need help to realize that it is possible and intellectually respectable for the Christian to have another answer. This help is needed by the young Christian to avoid spiritual difficulties growing out of unbelieving philosophies; directed toward the non-Christian it is a sort of evangelism.

This third argument is not subject to the criticisms directed at the second. It clearly leaves room for individual growth and choice. It takes seriously the fact that in the recent past, contact with unbelief in public institutions of higher education has led sincere young Christians to shipwreck. Any criticism of the parochial approach to problems of education must deal seriously with this argument. At this point we must limit ourselves to the remark that the parochial high school is not by any means a sure solution to the problem. First of all, it is inadequate because such problems become burning only at a later age. They are more serious in college than in high school, and still more serious in graduate school. A sheltered high school experience, even if it provides the student with answers which satisfy him then, can never endow him with sufficient momentum to make the rest easier. It might in fact be made harder by the fact that the answers he was satisfied with at first turn out later to have been short cuts. This argument is inadequate further because the intellectual battle with unbelief is so far from being won that even if we were institutionally prepared to bottle-feed our young people with the right answers, we wouldn't have those answers. The institution is useless unless there are textbooks with adequate content and a different general orientation from that of the public schools. For this Harry Rimmer's books are a weak substitute.

Often the argument for or against parochial education is carried on under the presupposition of an economy of abundance. We ask whether such a school would be helpful or not "in itself," assuming that if it is useful the funds and personnel will be forthcoming. Here we must recognize that it is not the case theologically. If the Christian church is essentially missionary, charged with the evangelization of the whole world, a task of which she is incapable financially and personnel-wise, then no investment of personnel and funds can be justified "in itself." Stewardship does not mean putting to a good use whatever resources we have to spare; it means using all our resources for the best possible purpose. Resources used for one purpose cannot be used for another. It is thus quite conceivable that the church should have to say that even if, "in itself," a church-guided school system would be desirable (as would also a church-guided consumers' co-operative, a church-guided clothing store, a church-guided soil conservation service, a church-guided radio station . . .), the missionary situation and the poverty of the church in our time does not make it seem that the best possible investment of a sizable slice of our meager resources would be to build such a system.

Culture for Service

It is characteristic of our times to speak in global expressions such as "all of life," "the whole man." Both education and religion favor such terms, especially where the two attempt to coincide in Christian higher education, we hear statements to the effect that the peculiar task of a Christian college is to bring all of life within the scope of faith, to teach the student to see his every activity as related to his Christian commitment.

One cannot say that this attitude is wrong—it is in fact noble. But at the same time it is deeply ambiguous, for it fails to indicate what is meant by "all of life"; thus room is left for using the term simultaneously with two different meanings, the one cultural and the other personal. It does not necessarily follow, from the fact that Christian faith demands the consecration of the whole personality ("all of life"), that therefore all realms of cultural endeavor ("all of life"), can be brought within a Christian frame of reference. This is another point at which there is danger that our thinking be determined by presuppositions foreign to our faith. If it were assumed that all people are essentially alike and essentially good, then all realms of human activity can be christianized. If however, humankind is what the Bible calls "the world," and the first step in faith is to break with that world, then the culture accumulated through the centuries by that world is not necessarily all worthy of attention. The literature studied in a Christian college will not as a rule include pornographic literature, the athletics practiced on a Christian campus will either not be like other athletics or not be Christian.

We raise this question because of the strength of the forces leading toward conformity. It is somehow assumed that higher education is an autonomous realm with its own standards, so that a Christian institution should without question (if it is in that realm at all) seek to be authorized to give a valid diploma. Economics, literature, music, and history are fields of scholarship with their own norms, and the Christian scholar should be a leader in his field. There is presumably no field in which scholarship is not needed, and thus a Christian college should attempt to excel in all fields. The ideal for a Christian college, if we think in this direction, should be a full university.

However it may be that a certain amount of this openness to culture is desirable, especially for religious groups that in the past have avoided civilization in an unhealthy way, it must be seen that it is an attitude inherently devoid of standards, incapable of steering itself. The fundamental question is whether culture will furnish the standards for our service, or service the standards for our culture. Although the Christian's first reaction in theory would always be to say that service is the criterion of culture, the momentum of the institution and the tendency toward autonomy within each discipline, the importance of being accredited and granting acceptable degrees, create a constant slope toward conformity and a constant danger that culture itself will become the criterion for service.

A half-century ago, the typical Midwestern church-affiliated college had an ordained minister as its president and was directly supervised by some church authority. Chapel attendance and courses in Bible were compulsory. Dancing, dramatics, and the use of alcohol were forbidden. Today that typical college has chosen its president from the humanities or social sciences department of its faculty, the church connection has been loosened, chapel attendance is compulsory only once a week, the Bible course has been replaced by one in "religion," dances are a part of the program, and drinking is tolerated without being officially permitted. In short, the college, filling its place in American culture, has severed itself from its original spiritual intention because the norms of culture are all-powerful. Serious Christians remain on its faculty, just as they might be the employees of a state university, but the institution itself has ceased to consider itself as committed to Christian standards.

Since this development of the Christian college seems to be just as inevitable, sociologically speaking, as the "sect cycle," it would seem that considerable caution would be called for before accepting the thesis that an educational institution should be open to all of the surrounding culture and (as a corollary thereto) should seek to provide an education to all corners. Proposals for an alternative concept of the college's function shall be made later. For the present we need only to observe that the problem of the church's relation to the world, and the means of "holding the young people," is also to be met at this level. Discipline problems are common knowledge that arise from trying to enforce conservative behavior standards on young people who, whether they signed the entrance papers sincerely or not, are not personally convinced by these standards. What is not always recognized is that such difficulties, far from being abnormal, are the thing to be expected when the institution itself has not clearly decided between the church and the world. If the institution chose to be a work of the church, in the strict sense, and accepted only such students as sought to carry on their studies within a disciplined fellowship, or if it chose not to be a work of the church and met the ethical standards of its students halfway, such problems would not arise. They arise only when the conditions for admission and the conditions for discipline fail to correspond.

No good is done by oversimplifications, and it would be irresponsible to argue that a modified philosophy of education would eliminate discipline difficulties. Our only intention here has been to bring into focus two of the centers of concern with which either a philosophy of education or an institution must deal. One is the problem of culture; the other is that of the membership of the academic community. In both respects, our discussion begins with the recognition that these problems have not yet been solved, either in theory or in institutional practice.

2

A Syllabus of Issues Facing the Church College

(Pre-Workshop Paper, April, 1964)

JOHN HOWARD YODER

Introduction

I understand my assignment in the present paper to be that of raising issues rather than suggesting their resolution. Now an issue is live only if a case can be made for more than one possible answer. My task can therefore be more narrowly defined as demonstrating that there actually are issues concerning which it would be possible to arrive at different conclusions from those currently sustaining the church college. This will mean I shall be taking the role of "devil's advocate," giving more attention to the less popular side of any given debate.

At some points it may be possible for me to sketch the nature of an issue without taking sides at all; in other places the only way to make an issue come alive may be to argue for one possible solution. Even where such argument might represent my tentatively settled conclusion (which will not always be the case), the purpose of the argument is to open and not to close conversation on the issue.

One of the issues at stake is the very method of choosing which issues are important. Many analyses of problems of higher education come out with just one or two issues thought to be fundamental to the others. Any such selection of only one or two problems thought to be crucial would prejudge the evaluative process that we have just barely begun in preparation for next August's workshop. I shall therefore attempt to lay out a greater number of issues, classified but not sifted, leaving it to the study process of the larger community to determine which are the most challenging and promising.

One way to somewhat narrow our task will be to label some issues which, although quite important for the Christian's total intellectual experience, do not *necessarily* correlate with the institution of the church college. Often in the books I have been reading one finds discussions of the Christian's reason for wanting to "pursue the truth," as if "the pursuit of truth" were the best description of the undergraduate educational process; certainly a misunderstanding of what the college teacher does with most of his time. Similarly, discussions of the relationship between teaching and research, or of the theological assumptions that permit the Christian to be a scholar or a scientist, do not directly speak to whether the church should be operating colleges.

Issues Arising From the Passing of the Pioneer Age
The Job Well Done

The more precisely one defines the indispensable appropriateness and the unique creativeness of the frontier college, the more clear does it become that the situation which called forth that characteristic American institution has passed. From the opening of the Western territories to the First World War, a situation was made to order for the contribution that only such institutions could offer.

What needed to be done was to train the elite minority who would provide the cultural backbone of the transcontinental society coming into being. It was a task that could be done on a shoestring, with teaching methods and the curriculum hardly open to much variation. Bringing civilization to a continent was at the same time a vision of exhilarating magnitude, and a job which was going to have to be done by ordinary people doing what they knew how to do.

It is the very fact that this job was done by voluntary agencies which has changed the situation so that their contribution is no longer of the same nature. The effectiveness of their educating an elite was so great that now far greater numbers of young people must be served at the college and university level. Even without increasing specialization and the growing costs of libraries and laboratories, to operate on the needed scale would be financially impossible for voluntary agencies. It is the very vision of educational excellence fostered by the frontier schools at their best which set the pattern for a level of quality which they now find themselves hard pushed to provide for even a minority of the young people interested in college. It is thus a recognition of their achievement when the larger society, both through the instrument of the state and by the "secularizing" of the larger church-related schools, has provided institutions which will be doing the bulk of educating.

Now that it is clear that the task will be done one way or another and that society is not utterly dependent upon the churches' services, we need a whole new rationale if we are to be able honestly to make a case for what could be taken for granted in another age. Why now the church college?

(I indicated above that there are some concerns related to the Christian in scholarship that do not connect directly with the issue of the churches' call to support colleges. It is the mark of the embarrassment of some church college thinking at the present time that we find more discussion about the nature of truth and the Christian's obligation to be culturally creative, than about the central fact that the church college is an institution devoted to teaching young people of a certain age group certain types of curriculum material at the expense of church contributors. Most of the quite edifying things said in many of these standard works are not relevant to whether the church should continue to collect money for dormitories and libraries.)

The Loss of Churchly Character

Much commentary has been devoted to the phenomenon of "secularization" by which many colleges with an initial ecclesiastical commitment have moved gradually to a "general American" orientation, with [little] specific denominational or theological commitment.

I would submit that it is not as clearly out of order as some seem to assume when, with the merging of voluntarily sponsored higher education and socially sponsored mass education, the churchly character of the institution diminishes. In the withering away of explicit religious identification the colleges simply reflected the trend in American society at large, in which, coupled with a steady increase in church membership, the churchly meaningfulness of that membership has progressively diminished. If we are to express regret, it should be for this broader social phenomenon and not with the covert suggestion that perhaps the colleges were responsible for it. If on the other hand we recognize that the authority of the churches in that earlier age was more a reflection of the prestige of established religion in the European heritage than of the actual converted conviction of the American population, then we might not be so sure that the withering away of this deceptive churchly authority was clearly a setback. The churches were the founders of colleges not because of any deep theological drive, but because the churches were the only clearly organized structures of voluntary social initiative in the frontier society. They were not only church-related but denomination-related, not because any one denomination had a better theological reason for educating than another, nor because each denomination had a distinct educational message, but simply because the pluralistic denominational pattern is the pattern of voluntary social relationships. It is, in effect, our kind of "establishment." Those of us who are not specifically committed to the pattern of "established religion" should therefore not necessarily feel that the situation has fundamentally changed with the weakening of that type of official religious expression in the semi-public institutions which colleges always have been.

The Sectarian School

The awareness, made quite clear by Norman Kraus's paper—that the pluralistic denominational pattern was itself the religious establishment of the pioneer age, and that therefore the classical college pattern was not "church" alone but already an interaction of the church with the larger society—should sharpen our perception to distinguish from the church college not only the much more narrowly defined Bible Institute, committed only to the training of church worker, but also a third type, which

I should like to designate as "sectarian," without meaning this adjective in a pejorative sense.[1] The Ira Miller paper has, I think, made clear that the founding of Mennonite Colleges and the reorganization of Goshen College included an element of denominational identity and defense which was not typical of the classical church college pattern.[2] There can be in such an effort of a small minority group to maintain its identity through an educational program something defensive and anti-cultural, but this is by no means automatically the case. The degree of separateness and the particular identity of a denomination are not necessarily indications of being closed to the larger society or to general cultural values. Witness the abiding cultural creativity of Jesuit schools through the centuries. We shall have to study further whether the maintenance of sectarian identity in our society is either a possible or a desirable function of a church college; my only point at present is that we should be aware that this kind of function is something quite distinct from the grand tradition of the church college in American history.

Integral Constituency Loyalty

With the development of the "sectarian" pattern, it was to be expected not only that the admissions policies would tend to be tied rather closely to the denominational convictions, but that we would observe the development of two further assumptions: that every loyal member of the denomination should prefer the denominational institution, and that therefore the institution is duty bound to find facilities for all the denomination's children.

It is only within the last five years that it has come clearly to the attention of Mennonites that this pair of assumptions is no longer realistic for us. And if they are not realistic, then to be limited by them is

---

1. [C. Norman Kraus contributed a paper for the same workshop as Yoder's contribution. The topic of Kraus's paper was "A Historical Critique of Church Colleges in the United States." The text of Kraus's unpublished paper (14 pages plus 5 pages of footnotes) is available from the Mennonite Church USA Archives, Goshen College V-1-22. I am grateful to Al Meyer (former Director of the Mennonite Board of Education) and Dennis Stoesz for their assistance in locating this paper. Meyer was a participant in the 1964 workshop. —Ed.]

2. [See Ira E. Miller, "Beginnings in Mennonite Higher Education" (February 1964). Like the papers of Yoder and Kraus, Miller's unpublished paper was prepared for the workshop on the Church College which was held in August 1964. I am grateful to Meyer and Stoesz for their assistance in locating this paper. —Ed.]

in fact clearly wrong, since it means in effect disavowing any pastoral or educational responsibility for those who can go to non-church schools without forfeiting their church membership.

The assumption that integral denomination loyalty would be the ideal has a double negative effect once significant numbers of students are on non-denominational campuses. The students themselves feel that they are being accused of disloyalty, and unfairly so, for not having chosen a school which they were not sure they could afford and where they were not sure they could find courses meeting their need. The college on the other hand feels rejected because it has identified its reason for existence with its claim to serve the total membership of the denomination.

I submit that, whatever was the possibility in the past, the idea that a denominational college can or should serve all the educational needs of its constituency is now utopian. The assumption was of course never applied to any fields of graduate study, except, quite recently, to the seminary. It has already been formally given up in some other areas, such as agriculture and engineering, which we admit a small school cannot do equally well. It would seem to follow that we should free ourselves entirely from the idea of a formal obligation to meet all of a certain category of study needs, recognizing that the case for the college must be made on some other basis than this. When in spite of the exceptional vigor and quality of Mennonite educational leadership in the last two generations, and in spite of the greater than average need of the constituency to catch up in the field of educational services, fewer than half of our wage earners contribute regularly to church colleges and nearly half of our young people in college are in non-denominational institutions. We must govern our actual institutional services by a rationale which fits reality rather than making the case for them on the axiom of an identity between denomination and school which, if it ever fully existed, is hardly growing.

Issues Related to the Stance of the Church as a Missionary Minority

We have barely begun to spell out the implications for educational method of the Anabaptist vision of the church. The overwhelming bulk of thought and practice in this realm ever since Origen has been dominated by the assumption that the educational process is a function of the total christianized society, both in being sponsored by society at large and in being responsible to meet all the needs of Christendom. Although Bernard Ramm is a Baptist, his survey of historical figures in his *The Christian College in The Twentieth Century* is totally uncritical with regard to this "Christendom" assumption of the thinkers on whom he reports. Over against this historic prejudice, the awareness that the church is a minority and that its task is a missionary one are the keys to the definition of a new perspective.

The Strategy of the Missionary Minority Is Parsimonious

We cannot do everything, and should not assume that we should. Our concern is therefore not for completeness or for the ability to cover the gamut of possible good services to society, but to select the most necessary. We must realize that there are many good things that could be done with church resources that are still not the best use to make of them.

One of the standards of discrimination in parsimony will be a judgment as to what others are now capable of doing. The point is not that certain services are worthy of Christian concern and others are not, but that among those valid concerns we must select those which will be left undone if we do nothing about them. Certainly this would not today be a ground for insisting on a church contribution to higher education, as it was in another age.

A further standard for our parsimonious discrimination will be the question, "How much difference does it make to be Christian in this realm?" It has often been pointed out that the various intellectual disciplines vary greatly in the extent to which religious or metaphysical commitments color the treatment of the material. In the field of physics, mathematics, or logic, there can hardly be said to be an enormous difference between the viewpoints of Christians and those of other competent students. In history, ethics, or social work, the same could not be said. Emil Brunner has used the phrase, "law of closeness of relation," to identify this phenomenon. The closer an issue is to the center of man's wholeness, the more visible the impingement upon it of man's relationship to God, the more the treatment of that material will be distorted by man's selfishness and rebellion, and therefore the greater the distance will be between the Christian and the non-Christian. (We may have occasion to speak later about whether this means that the disciplines like physics are "Christian" or not; the point here is simply that Christians would stand to lose the least by learning their physics at the hands of non-Christians.)

Quite obviously, one of the dimensions of parsimony must be strictly economic—we cannot pay for everything we would like, and increased expenditure in one realm means proportionately less resources for other dimensions of the church's mission. But the reason for suggesting that the church would not need to be the main teacher of physics is not only that the cyclotron is expensive; it is that there is about the teaching of physics (or of mathematics, which needs no cyclotron) an objectivity that means we need to think twice before investing the church's meager missionary resources in this branch of education,

The Missionary Church Is Not Governed by the Same Sociological Laws That Apply to Closed Communities

It is not difficult to sociologically analyze the patterns of education and preservation of group identity in a non-missionary minority, such as Mennonites have been in the past. Nor is it difficult to analyze society as a whole. Both of these are, although in different ways, closed units. A missionary church however is neither a closed ethnic minority nor a total society, but rather an open edge minority that finds its vitality in the crossing of the border between itself and the larger society. In pointing out that this phenomenon would call for a completely different set of tools of sociological analysis, I mean to be speaking not only of sociology as a science, but more broadly of the amateur sociological insight which is part of any modern man and which plays a large part in the way an institution understands itself.

The uniqueness of the missionary situation can be seen in the fact that the major leadership within God's people, especially so at crucial periods, has come not from persons who were fully at home in the center of their society and tradition, but from marginal persons. Moses had the education of an Egyptian prince, the Apostle Saul/Paul was before his conversion both an exceptionally representative Pharisee and a beneficiary of the best of the Hellenistic culture of the Jewish diaspora. In fact the entire missionary expansion of the New Testament documents was the product not of Palestinian Jewish Christians but of Hellenists, most of them not part of the first church in Jerusalem.

Obviously, the covenant people run a risk in associating in this open way with society at large and in accepting leadership from persons who are themselves at home on the growing edge rather than in the bloodstream of the heritage. But this is a risk that the church that believes in the Holy Spirit cannot afford not to run. It would also have to be said of recent Mennonite history that its most creative forces have been those borne by individuals who, while by no means disavowing their own Mennonite traditions, found significant new stimulus in the encounter with the larger society, whether in non-denominational educational institutions or on some other level. Is it not precisely the process of growth in the face of challenge that is stimulated especially by study in a "foreign" spiritual environment that produces this vitality? Are we not then cutting off one of the major sources of our needed renewal when we attempt to "grow our own" leadership? And when we try to guard our best youth against the public university?

Education Is not a Function of the Family

Closely related to the above paragraph, and also to the earlier discussion of the assumption of integral loyalty, is the concept of education as basically a function of the family, a responsibility of parents for their children. As self-evident as the idea that education is a family function seems when we think of the 3 R's, it by no means remains self-evident beyond that hypothetical point which we refer to as "the age of accountability," especially if we go on to the levels of education which actually presuppose that the student is practically an adult in intellectual capacity and mental independence.

In American society this assumption has been subject to challenge from two sides. First, it has been challenged by that of democratic ideology, according to which there is a common core of national, moral, and intellectual consensus that no group particularism should keep a child from learning about. On the other hand, less clearly articulated but intrinsically just as basic, would be the implication of believers' baptism that each individual must make his own ultimate decision regardless of the home in which he was placed by the accident of his birth.

But then are there other options than the concentration upon educating one's own children? Certainly there have been in other cultures. It is possible to concentrate on educating those who need it most. In past history Christians have always been exceptionally concerned for those whose class or racial origin prevented their receiving even a minimum of education. But perhaps more challenging in the welfare society to which we look forward would be the idea of concentrating upon those who will benefit most from an education, namely the most capable students and those likely to constitute the elite of the coming generation. From the Brethren of the Common Life during the Middle Ages through British Quakerism in the last two centuries, to the College Cevenol founded by Andre Trocmé, nonconformist Christians have demonstrated themselves capable of providing an education which parents who do not share their convictions were willing to purchase at cost for their children. Certainly if our concern is for mission rather than for self-preservation, then the suggestion that we might concentrate on educating the most educable, those most likely to constitute a future elite, and those who do not come from our own church circles, should have more to be said for it than we have thought of in the past. In addition to its obvious missionary challenge, such an approach would automatically avoid the objections against "indoctrination" which arise when a minority group teaches only its own progeny.

The Pioneer and the Paradigm

If we have once got away from the idea of meeting all the needs of a given social group, even our own, and of measuring the goals toward which we extend our effort in function of their needfulness and with a view to stewardship of our creativity, then we shall find ourselves especially interested in experimentation and in the development of novel methods that Christians should be disproportionately able to cook up. The point would be not to do everything but to show what can be done. Christians used to run all the hospitals. Now that the state knows that the hospital is a good thing the church is ill-advised to concentrate on medical research. At one time the need is to develop schools, another time it is mental hospitals, or overseas service techniques. Each time the larger society gets the point, Christians should move on instead of being jealous about the ministries they have developed.

The Stability of Adolescence

When the church college movement began in the catechetical school of Origen, as well as when it began on the American frontier, it was terminal education. Even if the level of instruction were not far beyond that of a good modern high school, the students would upon the completion of their studies be ready for professional responsibilities.

We have spoken earlier about the social change which comes about when this level of education is made accessible to half of the population instead of to a small minority. Our point now, however, is that with the educational explosion, the terminal education of persons getting ready for major social leadership takes place in the mid-twenties, whereas the general college educational experience has become a sort of prolonged adolescence, with the school needing to compete for attention with courtship and sports. Or in those cases where the prospect of a job has already prescribed a total curriculum, or where the student is already making his living, his education is again cramped by that fact to the point that it can have no "liberal" dimension.

Elton Trueblood has suggested that there is no good reason for the churches to continue to concentrate on the segment of our population which is really the least disposed to give itself deeply to the educational process. If we are to look at education once again with critical parsimony, it might be suggested that there are two other levels on which much more could rather be done.

In the one direction, a strong case could be made for more church-related education on those age levels where the young person is still quite normally within the family context, namely grade school and junior high. Here the argument for education as a family responsibility is the most appropriate, as is the possibility of reaching all of the children of a family as against being limited to those who go on to college.

But Elton Trueblood's concern was rather for the older age groups, whose greater experience in practical affairs would give them a better basis for all kinds of general study, for which they would be likely to have more leisure time, and in which they would be less misled by unfruitful rebellion or by idle curiosity. Adult education has never been exciting in North America, but is this not precisely because we have downgraded it in comparison to the college? No one can imagine what might happen if we invested in adult education the quality of teaching personnel now being expended on adolescents—to say nothing of the economy in physical plant and the closer integration of the educative process with the local congregation which this could enable.

Issues Arising out of the Nature of the Church
The Church Is a Voluntary Community

The center of the Anabaptist objection to a close tie between church and state was not alone the impropriety of using physical force to influence beliefs. The deeper issue was rather the nature of human community. The church is a community defined by the commitment of those who voluntarily join its fellowship. Now there is little danger that on the scale of operations which is possible for Mennonites we should have in our colleges anything like the state in its impersonality and violence. We do however—unless we should take quite novel measures toward identifying church membership and the status of student—run a serious danger of confusion between two bases of voluntary community. For the commitment to seek an education in a church college is by no means the same thing as Christian discipleship. As a matter of fact, we take few measures in the process of registration to move toward such identification, as Wheaton or Nyack would.

Goshen College currently has approximately 5 percent of its student body testifying to no religious orientation, another 10 percent recording some non-Mennonite church preference, in many of which cases the commitment is not necessarily a very deep one, and no way of knowing how many of the remaining 85 per cent of nominal Mennonites are seriously ready to be taken up on their commitment to responsible church membership. I am not suggesting that these unconvinced persons should not be on the campus, but that we should find structures of voluntary Christian fellowship which recognize their freedom to not be functioning church members as long as they are not so committed, rather than artificially decreeing free-church patterns of fellowship, worship, and service. But when the question arises, as it has on numerous of our campuses recently, what the meaning of compulsory chapel can be in a church of the Anabaptist tradition, the threat which this question seems to evoke indicates that for some it would seem to cut at the very reason for existence of a church college. What then is the reason for existence of a church college in the Anabaptist tradition, if to accomplish its purposes it must make church attendance compulsory?

The Church Is a Community and Not a Hierarchy

In contrast to the patterns obtaining in European universities where the administration of the university arises directly out of the faculty and major offices are in fact often rotated around senior faculty members, the American college and university administration is a profession of its own, tending, for reasons whose historical appropriateness one cannot challenge, to take most decisions either to the sponsoring boards or to administrative staff, with only certain restricted areas of responsibility being given either to the faculty as a community or to the students. This is thus another point at which we find patterns of management in operation that would be more at home (recognizing the limitations of any analogy) in the state church than in the voluntary community. The New Testament church recognizes very clearly the need for responsible leadership, but that leadership is expressed in the name of the community, subject to the control of the community, by numerous individuals called from the community. The way in which lines of authority in American church colleges go back through administrative boards to denominational hierarchies thus gives reason for questioning whether they ever could be conceived of as themselves truly "communities" of learning.

The Wall of Separation

Reference to the Anabaptist conception of relation of church and state obliges me to give some note to the Great American Debate, if only to recognize how difficult it is to see one's way through to clear answers on the question of state support for schools.

Any survey of the discussion trips immediately over a host of paradoxes. American Free Churches of the Anabaptist tradition, while insisting upon formal separation of church institutions and state agencies, unblushingly use all kinds of indirect subsidies not only for public service institutions like hospitals, but also (in the form of tax exemptions and deductions) for worship and missionary activities. At the same time denominations whose creedal tradition would call for them to accept or even demand a close tie with the state tend to be more independent. It is the Presbyterians who sometimes reject hospital subsidies and the conservative Reformed and Lutheran groups who run their own schools at their own expense. Whereas Christian colleges, including those of the Historic Peace Churches, showed no special wariness about administering Defense Education Act loans, it was the large public institutions that first raised questions about the loyalty oath and the military context of the funds in question.

A similar set of contradictions arises when we compare not denominations but professions. On the personal level, it would occur to very few to feel that the integrity of a Christian school teacher is seriously hampered—at least in peacetime—by his working for a state university or a township high school, yet medical doctors greet the hint of a step in the direction of social support for medical costs as not simply unprofitable for them but somehow a moral affront. Yet on the institutional level the opposite is the case. We have had no qualms about our mission board operating hospitals for local political units nor about church institutions receiving government funds in large quantities for the building of hospital facilities; yet when it comes to colleges, we seem much more afraid of controls.

One of the sources of the confusion is the assumption that in America the Anabaptists were finally listened to, and that the separation of church and state called for by the United States Constitution is somehow clearly related to the demands made under the same heading by Free Churchmen from Tertullian to Roger Williams. By no means is this the case. The American Constitution provides for a pluralism of religious agencies, no one of which receives unique government recognition, but at the same time it continued to be assumed that the nation would be both pious and Protestant, and that the practice of religion would be favored in every way that would be found possible without favoritism. This is a kind of establishment.

It would be impertinent to think any brand new clarity could be suggested in a few lines. I therefore suggest that we first augment the confusion by getting over the idea that a simple set of alternatives has been drawn before us. We should not necessarily assume that a church college has the same reasons for being separate from the state as a church congregation or conference. For the college, after all, does render a public service and enable an economy for the state education budget, yet we have had no qualms about tax deductions and exemptions for our congregations.

If our concern in this matter is for spiritual independence, it should certainly not be assumed that a college dependent upon large amounts of funds contributed from nongovernmental sources would be spiritually freer. For all the major private sources of money are themselves political and ideological forces in the kind of society we have. Since in fact this money is his own, the American capitalist donor is more likely to attach strings to its expenditure than if he were a public functionary dispensing the resources of the whole community. The experience of universities in many other parts of the world, which have been able to continue as havens of intellectual and even political independence even within regimented societies, would indicate that it is not impossible to avoid over-control if the government funds received by a school can be institutionalized and thereby freed from the arbitrariness of passing political pressures.

Without having proposed an argumentation to make this conclusion inevitable, may I suggest that if a church-related college is serving a total society according to the ground rules of open society, then the services rendered in that institution have as much right to be paid for according to the current prices in that market as do the equally honest products of our farmers, who notoriously have not refused market prices simply because the market was federally manipulated. If on the other hand we are to make an increasing case for the institution as an arm of the church serving primarily the church by focusing primarily on the issues of faith and producing primarily church servants, then it would not only be a concern for spiritual autonomy but in fact for simple honesty which should lead us to raise questions about some of the indirect support we are already receiving, to say nothing of new types of grants.

Issues Arising out of a Concern for Radical Discipleship

It should not be necessary to spell out at great length the nature of the traditional Mennonite concern for radically serious obedience, even, if need be, at the cost of finding oneself unable to fulfill certain "police" functions which society cannot do without. We have applied this not only to military functions, but by and large to the use of the courts and to the legal profession as well. As we see the church moving far beyond the face-to-face community, we need to ask whether there might not be dimensions of this institutional reality which make the entire undertaking an unwise spiritual risk.

This would not mean to say that the use of powerful institutions would automatically be impossible for Christians—a sort of Franciscan reflex—the concern is again a pastoral and a parsimonious one, asking whether the particular risks are justified compared to other perhaps less perilous and more fruitful undertakings.

Personality Versus Community

The centralization of administrative discretion in one individual or a small circle, which with the very best of intentions cannot always consult everyone concerned in a decision, has already been identified above as one of the pitfalls.

The Tyranny of Curriculum

Once the decision has been made to offer a certain gamut of courses, a college administration has committed itself to a mechanism that it henceforth will be extremely difficult to resist. Staff will need to be employed to teach the courses which have been offered. These staff persons will be hired on the basis of their competence and their capacity to interest students. Certainly there will be great concern for their also being committed Christians and in fact Mennonites, but if the pressure is great this may not always be possible. If by "committed Christians" we should mean that average level of "benevolence toward the religious" which passes for Protestantism in America, or the passive conformity to patterns of nonconformity that passes for Mennonitism, the difficulty would not be too great. But if we say we are devoted to the recovery of the Anabaptist vision and the renewal of discipleship in our day, the chances that persons fitting our teaching needs will at the same time share our theology are actually rather slim, and grow slimmer as the institution grows. In another way as well, the curriculum's mechanism dilutes our witness. The need to provide a gamut of offerings corresponding to student needs means that a large personnel effort will be invested into teaching courses in which the teacher's being Christian makes little difference for the subject matter. By no means do I mean to say that a Christian cannot be a competent and objective biologist and still be a disciple. Nor do I mean to say that a Christian teaching biology will not leave a witness with his students in spite of the fact that the course material itself raises few moral issues. My point is that if we have a person whose gifts are such that while teaching biology he can be a witness, it is a shame to have urged him to enter that field because we need someone in the department rather than having him, with his gifts, in a place where the difference his faith makes would be more immediately evident.

The Administration of any Institution Is an Exercise of Power

The clarity with which Anabaptists rejected the physical sword has hidden from some of us an awareness of the "sword-likeness" of certain other kinds of social leadership, especially such as have to do with the allocation of money, with hiring and firing, and with who is and who is not consulted in a given decision. The heightening of these temptations does not make it a priori impossible to be meek and nonresistant in a position of responsibility, but they heighten the pressures on certain persons beyond the points which most mortals are able to resist. Some other Christian groups, notably the Quakers, have found peculiarly church-like patterns of administration to compensate for this difficulty; Mennonites have thus far not done so. We have not demonstrated creativity in finding brotherly checks and balances to control the powers given to certain brethren; nor have we demonstrated that spiritual independence of the affluent that is enjoined by the Epistle of James (chapter 2).

The Problem of Integrity

One of the subtle temptations in the ethical realm arises simply out of the size that demands a division of labor. Every institution (like every person) has a "philosophy" or set of objectives which govern its policy decisions, a set of objectives which serve for evaluation of its past performance, and a set of objectives to interpret itself to others. An individual only has integrity if the standards used in all these points are the same and if he is actually governed by and willing to be judged by what he tells people he is up to. When in an institution the making of general policy is located with the board, the doing of the teaching is delegated to the faculty, and the promotion to the public is the responsibility of the "relations" and the admissions offices, there is a built-in tendency toward unintentional duplicity. I have noticed in Mennonite colleges that our promotion offices can say things with great conviction which administrators are somewhat less sure of and faculty members still less. This would be no special problem for Christians of those traditions which have good theological explanations of a certain amount of compromise in good causes. It means something quite different within a tradition in which the transparent integrity of yes meaning yes and no meaning no has been an article of faith.

The Autonomy of the Secular

Every body of knowledge and therefore every academic discipline has its own set of truth and value clams. Since each of these disciplines has grown out of a history in which at one time all of the truth was thought to be a part of "Christian civilization" and since each discipline now operates with its own subject matter and outside the bounds of the religious community, it is obvious that some of the truth and value claims of the several academic disciplines will "reach over" into the realm of Christian convictions. This is the problem which has been referred to by means of the slogan, "Jerusalem or Athens?"

The Autonomy of "Athens"

It goes without saying that one of the possible solutions to this problem is to affirm that each realm of intellectual and creative endeavor is fundamentally autonomous, finding in its own subject matter a standard of truth which is all that should guide it. Some of this concern comes from unpleasant experiences with authoritarian defenders of the faith whose conviction seemed to lead them into disregard for the facts or for the responsibility of their colleagues. Another source of this concern for autonomy has been the necessity for the graduate student, whether artist or scientist, to accept the value system of the community in which he acquires his expertise if his own competence is to receive recognition. Still another basis is the simple encounter with the objectivity and dignity of each of the several realms of creativity and investigation.

It is thus not surprising that the main streams of church history have found ways to affirm a relative autonomy for the various elements of "secular" civilization, and that some have gone farther to affirm that this autonomy is fundamental. Sometimes it is affirmed as a matter of faith that recognizing the autonomy of the arts and sciences will lead to no conflict but rather to a happy synthesis, such as the Middle Ages or the person of Cardinal Newman are assumed to represent. At other points, the vision is rather that of a continuing fundamental tension between deeply differing views of truth which however must both continue to receive our loyalty; this would be the attitude of a Reinhold Niebuhr. For still others, there can be a clear division of labor such that each value system is master in its own field, and each, including Christian, commitment should stay in its own area and make no broader claims.

Each of these proposed solutions is open to serious challenge. That which claims autonomy for each realm on the basis of a doctrine of creation, which one tends to find in both Lutheran and Calvinistic circles, involves a misunderstanding of the biblical doctrine of creation as in no way standing over against redemption and especially as certainly giving to the creature no autonomy over against the divine will.

The "continuing tension" solution, although apparently quite honest and open to the facts, is in reality not fully responsible. For although tension can be a continuing psychic state, in the realm of scholarly and artistic productivity something is still going to be produced and in each case the tension will have been resolved by a commitment in a given case to one side or to the other or to a mixture in certain proportions, which is then no longer an active tension but a settled resolution.

Nor is the idea of "each in his own camp" a solution. It might suffice if our only need were to keep the physicists out of the music studio and the poets out of the laboratory. Even here it would not be easy. But the disciplines of history and psychology, to say nothing of theology and philosophy, have precisely as their specific bailiwick the entire breadth of human experience; any attempt to affirm that there are specific realms in which they must not go, although affirming the integrity of those other realms, denies the integrity of history or theology. Since it is the theological issue which concerns us now, we must note that any of these ways of affirming the autonomy of a given discipline, by claiming to know in advance that the Christian faith either cannot or must not have anything to say in that area which would differ from the convictions of the specialists, constitutes a serious challenge to the biblical and Anabaptist confession of the Lordship of Christ. How is autonomy different from rebellion? If a given realm is not subject to the Lordship of Christ what are we doing there? This kind of argument surprises us by beginning with the claim that all of life should be the Christians' concern, but concluding that the only honest way to be concerned with it is so to respect the independence of every area that his faith is not relevant to it.

Solutions Which Deny the Problem

It is no surprise that there is a reaction, over against this autonomy claim, which hopes by virtue of formal statements of faith to be able to deny that the problem is there. Behind such slogans as "truth is one" or "discipleship is all of life" or "no part of God's world can be closed to His children," it is hoped that with a sufficiently pious or sufficiently technical prior orientation the problems can be brushed away. All of these slogans are formally true. The difficulty is that they are also without clear meaning. For they do not give clear instructions as to what is now to happen when there is an *apparent* conflict. I grant that partisans of this "unity" vision may well hold that the conflict is only apparent, but how now do they resolve it? Some could without denying any of the above slogans take the most "secularist" line currently being advocated by a number of best-selling theologians, according to whom it is precisely this vision of unity that will permit us to drop all of the pious trappings of earlier Christian culture without really losing anything.

On the other hand, the same vision of unity can lead to the Christian syntheses of Abraham Kuyper or medieval Catholicism in which it was assumed that all the freedom the arts and sciences could reasonably want would be within the limits of a permanently fixed creed.

Beyond its lack of precise operational meaning, the "truth is one" theme does not speak to the issue of a Christian college. That idea that "Christians may well go into any realm" does not yet tell us what they should do there. That there is something constructive for them to do in every realm, even if guaranteed—and we have not been too sure of that about some realms—does not yet demonstrate that what should be done there is to operate an instructional program for youth between seventeen and twenty-three at church expense. Bernard Ramm's book providing a helpful historical survey of what Christian educators have thought about their subject matter is of no help with the description of the proper institutional base for the Christian teacher. It does not explain why he should not, like Melancthon or Moberly, teach in a state university.

Limited Autonomy

Nor is Bernard Ramm clear on the larger question we are now discussing. At times one would have the impression that he ascribes some independent value to the several "secular" disciplines. Yet at the same time that he reports on Augustine's great freedom in incorporating Roman rhetorical equipment into the education of priests he says that these pagan disciplines need to be "converted." Similarly in the discussions of Melanchthon and Kuyper, the idea that all secular disciplines may be used and the idea that they must be critically sifted to avoid all error run side by side without any clear guidance as to what to do in cases of conflict.

The historical survey by Norman Kraus made it clear that this is one fundamental issue facing the church college, and which liberal arts colleges in the past centuries have failed to resolve. What is the truth value of the course content in which the discipline itself comes forward with truth claims on subjects where Christians thought they had other kinds of reasons for holding to other ideas? When the artist, claiming that his only responsibility is to portray "what he sees," produces a picture which Christians feel offends either their taste or their morals, is the answer that he does not belong in the church? Or that he should be left to follow the dictates of his own "gift?" When the biologist reports that whatever the actual course of events in distant time might have been, he and his colleagues can only communicate meaningfully about inter-relatedness of organic life by positing an evolutionary hypothesis, is he to be told that be may "believe in evolution" only so far as he affirms it to have been a tool of theistic creation? Or that he may use it as a hypothesis but not as a truth? Or that whatever he believes in the field of biology has nothing to do with faith? And if the latter path should be taken, will we grant to the psychiatrist for whom morality is simply a projection of unhappy childhood experiences, or to the behaviorist, for whom all religious experiences can be reduced to chemical reactions in brain cells, the same green light? It is very easy to say that our teaching of every subject is penetrated by Christian faith. As long as this means that we open our classes with prayer, or that we gratefully receive the material of our discipline as part of a gift to us from a friendly God, this poses no problem for course material. But the Christian truth claim is really only meaningful if it does pose problems on the levels of truth and value—problems to which neither systematic subordination nor fundamental autonomy can provide a satisfying Christian answer.

The Superiority of Liberal Arts
The Utility of the Non-Utilitarian

The author of the study, *Piety and Intellect at Amherst College*, reports that when with the relaxation of sectarian loyalty there developed on the campus a conflict between the advocates of "piety" and the friends of "learning," the best way found to avoid open conflict was to concentrate on "character," on which the classicists and the devout can agree.[3] This remark is a pointer toward a much more general phenomenon. In the case of embarrassment arising from the absence of a clearer rationale for the educational process as it is now being carried on, whether this embarrassment relates to the growing autonomy of the secular just referred to, or derives from some of the broader sociological challenges

---

3. Thomas Le Duc, *Piety and intellect at Amherst college, 1865-1912* (New York: Columbia University Press, 1946).

now facing the church school, resort is often had to the superior moral value of "general education" or the "liberal arts."

Many contemporary discussions of the meaning of liberal arts read into this phrase numerous most edifying descriptions of what it means that the Christian is "truly free" or how the study of classical literature "liberates" one. Only a few have the honesty to admit that the historic derivation of the term is a quite different one. The "liberal arts" were originally those arts in which the leisure class of society could afford to indulge. Their first value was that they provided the kind of non-utilitarian occupation with which it was seemly for persons of their class to be busied. A second value was that they could thus actually preserve and propagate a classical humanistic heritage for which there was at the time not much other use. Further, the structure of their society being what it was, this training was for them utilitarian in that it prepared them to continue to be the kind of social elite that their parents were.

Now that many other kinds of professions have found ways to make themselves more efficient through the formal schooling of future professionals, upper-class reflexes have reacted against "mere training" as being something less than education. Especially when this "training" is in fields which are immediately useful, such as dietetics or accounting, many would argue that this should not be considered as education at all.

Interestingly, the critics of "mere training," although in agreement at this point, soon diverge rather radically. On the one hand there are those who would abandon dietetics and accounting in favor of the pure sciences because of their greater ultimate usefulness; seeking utility after all, but on a higher level. Others would at the same time make a still stronger case for sciences which are truly "pure" in that they are not justified by their contribution to technology, classical languages which simply teach one to think straight about his words, and of course the arts, whose claim to higher cultural value is that they are not good for anything else.

This general bourgeois cultural reflex takes on a new dimension when it is argued that it is specifically Christians who for "religious" or "character building" reasons should be concerned especially for the liberal arts. For a surprising number of interpreters, the case for a Christian college is identical with the case for a liberal arts college (and usually with the case for a small college). Such things as "perspective" or "cultural breadth and depth" are assumed to be more faithful reflections of religious concern than merely learning to be useful.

The Corrective of Discipleship

I submit that this glorification of the gratuitousness of character formation is not only morally questionable but in fact not an accurate description of what the Christian schools have been doing. The liberal arts curriculum, in the first place, was generally established because of its usefulness in preparing persons for the Christian ministry and the other professions. Christian colleges have always placed strong emphasis on the preparation of workers for the service professions, and have justifiably pointed to the disproportionately large number of nurses, doctors, teachers, church servants, and social workers whom they have prepared.

But even if there had been a history of Christian commitment to purely useless liberal arts, we would need from the Anabaptist perspective to challenge it seriously. We should challenge the social situation in which there was in the first place a leisure class. We should challenge the assumption that a drifting adolescent has more character than someone who has already set his sights on a way to be useful to his brethren and neighbors. We should recognize that even within a liberal arts curriculum there needs to be choices about the relative usefulness of different types of studies, to which process of discrimination the glorification of the non-utilitarian makes no contribution. We would further suggest that it is not only morally but also pedagogically preferable to build "character" around preparation for a clearly defined social task than for its own sake.

The Abiding Necessity of Liberal Arts

Once we have freed the liberal arts from the handicap of the case some have been attempting to make for them, we can see more clearly to define their real utilitarian necessity. Some would say that general education is preparation for "citizenship." If this means preparation for effective participation in democratic self-government, there might be some question about its adequacy as a motivation. If however we were to take the term in the broader sense of a responsible contribution to the *civitas*—that is, a competent contribution to social usefulness and leadership—then we could see quite clearly what each of the elements of general education can add, and we could judge this contribution and re-evaluate our curriculum with a vision toward whether we are actuality producing persons of this most useful type. Instead of saying that general education has no specific professional usefulness, we would ask for which callings it is professionally necessary.

I am not ready to guess what this partial shift of definition would do to our liberal arts curriculum. My suspicion is that it might move the general education courses from the level of undergraduate requirements for persons who are obliged to dilute their job training with a study of civilization and music appreciation which they shall hasten to forget, to the status of an upper-level concentration on the humanities as an arena of moral conflict and testimony, but this is only a guess.

It should be said with regard to liberal arts, as it was earlier in connection with the unity of truth, that the case for this kind of education is not identical with the need that today it should be offered by a church institution. In fact, there is something about the autonomy of the contemporary cultural materials that one must study in this field which it is practically impossible to present truthfully in a church context.

The Need for an Appropriate Philosophy of Education

The Synoptic Approach

Most of the effort to give the educational process an undergirding and theoretical understanding has proceeded by the synoptic path. The effort has been to begin with as broad a view as possible of the world at large and to place in it every realm of human effort and thereby every realm of education. This tends to assume the possibility of viewing the universe as a coherent unity that it is possible to get into focus, and a great variety of identifiable materials that it is possible to classify. Just recently at Goshen College we heard a recognized expert in the field of philosophy of education demonstrate what he conceives as his task as a philosopher to be. He did not intend to tell us what to teach and not what not to teach, and he left to one side the entire field of applied learning, to concentrate on classifying the several areas of general education within a chart, ordering them in terms of varying degrees of "intension" and "extension." In some of the areas on the chart "facts" are being dealt with, and it was not apparent that the Christian would have toward these facts any fundamentally different attitude from the conscientious and intelligent non-Christian. On other levels, value was being dealt with, and here religion was at home. From this perspective then, theology and ethics will look back over the realm of fact and be interested in it as part of a coherent worldview. The concern in setting up the synopsis was thus not for discrimination between what belongs and what does not belong in a Christian educational process but for "topology" which can get every item on the map and elucidate the relatedness of the various areas.

This is not to challenge either the helpfulness or the accuracy of the synoptic and descriptive approach to some kinds of problems. Yet the very effort to relate Christian faith to such a realm by transmuting it into a "worldview" or value system denatures it. Christian discipleship is not a worldview or a value system capable of objectively englobing everything and putting each item in its place. Christian faith is rather a stance within history capable of testifying to any world and therefore to any worldview, but settling on none of the available options, judging them all for their pride, which is reflected precisely in their claim to be able to provide a synoptic vision, and offering to all the grace of regeneration which means death to self-concern and sloughing off of much that seemed valuable.

A Kerygmatic Philosophy of Education

What is said above is not meant to suggest that we could somehow excise the realm of "philosophy of education." The need is rather to develop in this field as in every other an understanding of what we are doing which is more radically faithful to the nature of the gospel and less subject to ontological Constantine temptations.

I am here suggesting that "proclamation" would be one key to the interpretation of what we should be doing in education, and especially in the field of "general education." By "proclamation" I do not mean primarily or exclusively the appeal to individuals to make an initial faith commitment. Very seldom if ever could such an appeal be responsibly structured into the educational process without doing violence to some element of that process. What we can and should do, however, is to proclaim to the world at large that the Lordship of Christ extends to the meaning of history, to the dignity but also the brokenness of human beauty, to the objectivity and also to the self-centered distortions of the human search for "truth." There would be proclamation in the fact that we would not only claim to be free of artificial restraints and able to move into the several realms of human creativity, but much more deeply that we would claim to have the tools of moral and humane discrimination to know which of the efforts in each of these realms is truly free, truly human, truly useable in the kingdom cause. To proclaim the judgment of all human efforts in Christ and their fulfillment in Him is a far different message from the under-handed glorification of creaturely autonomy which some mean when they read, "I am the truth" or "the truth shall make you free."

A Philosophy of Servanthood

Christians, and especially Mennonites, should have less of a guilty conscience than some of us have seemed to have in recent years about the "utilitarian" dimension of education. Since we cannot meet all needs of all people, let us discipline ourselves more severely to meet with real efficiency those needs for which no one else is prepared. Let us verify our assumption that teaching and nursing and pastoral leadership call for spiritual orientation and motivation which no other training institution can provide. If this can be demonstrated (and I am not saying whether I think it can) then let us have no apology for being "lopsided" in our choice of the professions for which we train.

Conclusion

My assignment was not to have a conclusion. To set forth the clear thesis that the church college as it now exists is bad stewardship, reflects a defensive and non-missionary vision of the church, denies the New Testament-Anabaptist vision of radical, nonresistant, flexible discipleship, and should therefore be abandoned, would be to short circuit the study process which we are just beginning. But for the study to be serious it should be recognized that this would be one possible conclusion, and that the logic leading in this direction finds its impetus not in a critical observation of any one institution, but rather in the very way the church colleges have been making their own case.

I have intentionally kept out of this discussion any attention to possible alternative patterns of higher education, such as the Conrad Grebel College approach, the systematic infiltration of university campuses, or a stronger focus on congregational education. I have looked only at the type of church college represented by our three institutions and their history, identifying the serious questions which arise out of this very history as to the adequacy of the explanations we have been giving ourselves for the last thirty years for the necessity of doing what we are doing as we are doing it. This does not mean I am pessimistic about the possibility of other and better reasons for doing something similar, but it has not been my task to suggest them.

3

Theological Statements for a Philosophy of Mennonite Education

John Howard Yoder
and Paul M. Lederach

The attached document is a specialized piece with a specific purpose. It was developed as a background for a philosophy of Mennonite education. The writers of the document are concerned that it should be understood and evaluated with this purpose in view.

It is not intended as a comprehensive confession of faith. Thus the materials and themes from the realm of theology were not selected with a view to balance or completeness as a doctrinal system. Instead it is an attempt to include topics which are capable of being given operational significance for thinking about education. If readers note the absence of important theological topics, we would wish to know what significance these topics have for the structure of an educational process.

Because of this concern for functional relevance, the document in a number of places deliberately avoids the use of theological language. This does not mean that we reject theological concepts, but that we are trying to express relationship between God and man and between man and man in language which may meet on common ground the language of educational philosophy and principles.

Because of a concern for brevity, these statements omit significant reference to many important biblical themes and/or persons. The selection of Abraham as the representative father of the faithful, for instance, leaves aside certain other points which could be made more fully if Moses, David, and the prophets were also given extended attention. The interest in Abraham as a model grew in part out of the history of this research process and the persons involved in it. However, we believe it can be justified on the grounds of similar references to Abraham in the New Testament. The statements have been refined during two workshops arranged by the Philosophy of Christian Education Research Committee. They have been further refined by a mail consultation with a representative group of Mennonite theologians.

I. THE NATURE OF BIBLICAL FAITH

A. God is at work in history creating for himself a people.

1. The Bible deals with history and its meaning, not with detached philosophical speculation, with events and not timeless theory, with obedience and met disincarnate ideals.[1]

B. The creation of the covenant people is a work of the grace of God. It is done for this people, in spite of the people's inability to meet its own needs.

1. Abraham is spoken of as the father of all believers because, like all persons of faith since him, he answered the call of God to become part of his people.

    a. Abraham forsakes security and lives toward the future.

    b. Abraham forsakes the unity of pagan society and civilization as given to him by the past and commits himself to a pilgrimage with God, not knowing exactly what is promised to him, but trusting God both for the certainty and goodness of the promise.

    c. Abraham is called out of the confusion of Babel, the fragmentation and conflict which human pride has brought down as judgment on a self-seeking society, and commits himself to becoming the father of a new community.

---

1. The Bible contains, and is also the source of, propositional truth of significance for man in every relationship.

d. Abraham accepts a new kind of life, in which he responds by faith to the promises and demands of the covenant. These demands are not opposed to his own welfare but are the means whereby God will bless him.

e. The ultimate promise given to Abraham is that through him the nations of the world shall be blessed.

C. God's creation of a covenant people is for the purpose of reconciling all things and all men with himself. To this end Jesus Christ is both the fulfillment of God's promise to Abraham and the initiator of a new covenant which is intended to include all mankind.

1. Jesus Christ is spoken of as the founder and perfecter of the faith because in his person the meaning of obedience to the call of God is realized.

    a. By his birth into the human condition.

    b. By his ministry to every dimension of the needs of men.

    c. By his death at the hands of rebellious men and for their sake to free them from the power and penalty of their rebellion.

    d. By his victory over death in the resurrection and ascent to the right hand of God.

    e. By his promised return to fulfill all God's purposes.

D. The same faith which sees God at work creating a people trusts him to fulfill his purposes in the future.

1. God is proclaimed to be in control of the course of history which will ultimately be brought to the fulfillment of the purposes he has set.

2. God intervenes in the experience of societies and of individuals, altering the course of events for his purposes.

E. The same God who calls and creates the people is proclaimed the Creator of all things. (We understand creation in the new creation—Jesus Christ and the new community, a fulfillment of the Old Testament's testimony to the Creator.) Creation, then, as the work of God who is calling men into covenant, is seen as a purposive act of God's grace and goodness.

1. When God created all things, he declared them good. All knowledge is first of all God's, all truth is his, all of man's activity is under his lordship.

    a. Man is given dominion or responsibility over nature. It is his responsibility to use it for God's purposes.

    b. Man is created male and female. Sexuality and the structure of the family into which man is born and within which he becomes himself are God's provision of the creation of personality.

    c. As Adam was first assigned the task of giving names to the animals, it is the function of man to discern meaning in the created world; to accumulate and interpret knowledge.

    d. The ordinary materials of life, food and drink, money, and social relationships, are the objects of the concern of God. There is no "secular" realm beyond the scope of his will.

2. Man's rebellion—which can also be spoken of as his subservience to Satan—has so distorted God's creation that it becomes his prison.

    a. Instead of exercising dominion of nature he makes it his idol.

    b. Sexuality and the family structure become perverted into sexuality and self-seeking indulgence.

    c. Knowledge is perverted into pride.

    d. Man attempts to put God in a compartment by the perverted use he makes of the distinction between the sacred and the secular in order to maintain his rebellious freedom in the rest of his life.

    e. Sin is not merely a metaphysical entity but the historical reality of the rebellion of man, his limited capacity for good and bondage to evil, known theologically as "depravity."

II. THE NATURE OF THE CHURCH AND THE MEANING OF MEMBERSHIP

A. The covenant people exist as a reconciled and reconciling community and live in fellowship with God and with one another.

1. To be a people is to have a common history. Israel looks back to how God had led Abraham and their fathers into Egypt, then through Exodus to Sinai and into the promised land. Christians look back to the life, death, resurrection, and ascension of Christ, to the gift of the Holy Spirit and to his continued working in their midst.

2. Christians gather in testimony to the past action of God; their worship is commemoration and celebration of that past action.

3. Christians gather with confidence in the continuing action of God. When past faithfulness of God is commemorated and proclaimed, when Christians give and receive counsel, bind and loose, and renew their commitment to common obedience, then Christ is truly present in their midst.

4. Since the present and future action of God is in continuity with his actions in the past, the Bible, which is the testimony to that past action, is the criterion for faithfulness of God's people in the present and the future. The church receives the Bible as the Word of God and the authoritative guide to faith in Christ and the life of discipleship.

5. The church is not, as Israel was not, a "club" of individuals with similar interests who freely or arbitrarily gather together under their own initiative and power.

6. The church is not, as Israel was not originally called to be, a "nation" defending her identity like her pagan neighbors through the power of kingship after the Canaanite model.[2]

---

2. "Israel" is here seen as a prefiguration of the church, which is only one of the meanings of the term. There are other perspectives from which Israel (ancient Israel or Judaism since Christ) can be viewed. These other views, however, do not have other implications for the meaning of membership in the church.

7. As the first fruits of the new humanity the church is to be God's servant and witness to his purposes for all creation and for all mankind. It is the society of the redeemed where his will is done through the renewing power of the Spirit and Word.

B. Membership is a matter of free adult decision.

1. Only "believers" (i.e., those who admit their need, renounce their past, and commit themselves to Christ and the church) are baptized. Persons are to be genuinely free to make this decision.

2. Infants are not baptized. The decision to be baptized requires awareness of the options, the sense of responsibility that goes with maturity, and a commitment to obedience to carry through the implications of that decision.

3. Religious liberty is assumed and social coercion is rejected. The church must be so structured that persons may freely enter on the basis of faith in Christ and a commitment to discipleship. Those who reject these should be free to leave the church, though not without earnest warning.

4. Social freedom (from coercion) and psychological freedom (awareness of options) are not intrinsic to the human situation. They are enabled only by the grace of God. Apart from this call, man is unfree, a slave of sin. The biblical/Anabaptist call for social and psychological freedom of choice must be distinguished from modern views of the innate moral freedom of man apart from God.

C. Membership is sharing within the life and fellowship of the congregation.

1. The Lord's Supper commemorates the work of Christ with the emblems of a common meal.

2. Members of the congregation commit themselves to the practice of mutual aid as each has need.

3. Members share in the exercise of the gift of ministry of each member for the upbuilding of the whole body.

4. Membership is total: every segment of life can be the subject of common interest and responsibility and a matter of common congregational concern.

D. Members of the congregation support one another with "binding and loosing"; with mutual admonition and forgiveness.
   1. The congregation finds the will of God in common study and counsel with preaching, teaching, shepherding, and correction.
   2. The congregation experiences and communicates reconciliation and forgiveness.
   3. The congregation applies the guidance of Scripture, seeking and testing its meanings for the present, in conversation with the Christian brotherhood.
   4. The congregation becomes the focus of the voice of the Holy Spirit for discerning God's will for the lives of its members.

E. Membership is participation in congregational mission.
   1. All members are engaged in the mission of the congregation; there are not two classes of membership, mature missionary members and ordinary members.
   2. Each member exercises his special gifts in the support and advance of congregational witness. (See Section IV for further explication of mission.)

III. THE MEANING OF DISCIPLESHIP AS RELATIONSHIP TO JESUS CHRIST

A. The disciple turns away from other values to serve Christ.
   1. This may include forsaking genuine values ("hating father and mother"), for the sake of a higher calling.
   2. One must turn away from all unworthy values: from those which pride or sensuality or paganism would absolutize.
   3. This calls for simplicity of life and vigilance in order to avoid becoming enslaved.

4. This may call for total rejection of certain pagan patterns, in which idolatry is discerned (graven images in the Old Testament, sacrifice to the image of Caesar in the New Testament).
5. In other cases the believer may rescue cultural values from idolatry and be enabled to use them without becoming their slave (the New Testament's acceptance of eating meat offered to idols, the Old Testament pattern of temple music).

B. The disciple obeys Jesus Christ as master.
1. For Christ to be Lord means that he receives the disciple's exclusive loyalty. All other values must be defined in terms of relationship to him.
2. Every dimension of life belongs within this obedience: there is no realm which is ruled by other standards.
3. For Christ to be Lord means that the disciple seeks to obey his "hard sayings," even when the full reason for them is not immediately evident, and even when it is not clear what "effectiveness" his obedience will have.
4. For Christ to be Lord means that his disciples take up "the cross." They follow his pattern of life and his verbal teaching: in the renunciation of honor, wealth, security, falsehood, and violence.

C. The Holy Spirit makes real the life of Christ in the life of the believer.
1. To become a disciple of Christ can be spoken of as regeneration, new birth, or conversion: the gift of a new nature and will and direction.
2. The life of discipleship can be spoken of as sanctification, holiness, growth in conformity to his nature and will.
3. To live as a disciple demands a continuing recognition of one's own inadequacy: "yieldedness" in continuing recognition of one's need for grace. The believer confesses that need and renews his commitment to obedience.

D. The disciple of Jesus Christ is, like his master, the servant of his neighbor.
   1. The servant is guided by the need of the neighbor.
   2. Cultural activity is not for selfish enjoyment or an end in itself, but for God and the neighbor.
   3. Self-giving, suffering love is at the heart of service. The way of the cross is the alternative to lordship (nonresistance).
   4. The servant serves his neighbor by transparency and truth, by telling rather than by manipulating. (The rejection of the oath.)

IV. THE MISSION OF THE CHURCH

A. The church is dispersed.
   1. The church is cosmopolitan rather than being identified with provincial interests, yet the local congregation seeks to be relevant and understood in its own situation.
   2. The concern of the church is cosmic: every area of creativity belongs to her mission in the world.
   3. The Christian is a pilgrim: he does not attach himself permanently to any place or culture; he lives in a voluntary minority community in a pluralistic society, in several overlapping communities or "worlds."

B. In the midst of the world, the church as the first fruits of the new humanity is different from the world.
   1. The uniqueness of the church will show in creativity in finding new ways of meeting needs, in "pilot" service to the larger society.
   2. The church discerns and judges idolatry. She seeks to bring every kind of mental perception into subjection to Christ.
   3. The church does not seek nor share sovereignty in the wielding of the sword among men.
   4. Through her obedience to Christ the church testifies to the world concerning the meaning of this call.

C. The church calls men to response.
   1. The message is not herself, but the heralding of the good news that God loves men and gave his Son for them.
   2. She calls individual men to repentance and faith and to enter her new community.
   3. She calls men to bring forth fruits worthy of repentance.
   4. This call must be communicated in many ways: in words and deeds, in formal preaching and teaching, in unplanned questions and comments and fitting silences, in prophetic witness and in communal solidarity.

D. The church discerns the meaning of what God is doing in history.
   1. She discerns his work of warning and judgment against idolatry and brutality and pride.
   2. In performing the tasks described above she discerns the possibilities of building a relatively better order of society and calls upon men within the institutions of society to lead and modify these institutions in the interest of the welfare of man and in line with the divine standards of human welfare.
   3. At the same time, she denounces the pretensions of men that their social achievements, even if they be "relatively better," can be identified with God's righteousness and recognizes that God calls on all to repent and experience his renewing grace and transforming power in Christ.
   4. She recognizes that what God is doing in history will culminate in a new heaven and a new earth of God's own creation, and that all men are subject to a final judgment.

V. **SUPPLEMENTARY STATEMENT ON CHILDHOOD AND PERSONHOOD**

   A. The question to which this statement seeks to speak:
      1. The cultural stream which we refer to as humanism has ever since the Renaissance augmented in many ways the weight of the concept of the individual "self" as a focus of values and duties.

2. Many developments arising out of the study and management of educational processes, and from psychology, have led to understandings of learning and growth as gradual, progressive, with no clear lines between childhood and adulthood.
3. Developments in religious education (of many different types, including "child evangelism") have underlined how widely the young mind may be influenced, and what a variety of "religious experiences" young persons are capable of under certain circumstances.
4. Developments in Mennonite self-understanding, by lifting up the "believers' church" character of the Anabaptist church type, have raised questions about the ways in which revivalism and child evangelism have tended to lower the age of baptism. These and other considerations called forth the decision, in the 1968 workshop, to assign for drafting two topics in this realm: one on the self and self-fulfillment, and another on the nurture and the religious experience of the child. This draft now attempts to speak to both of those areas, since they are closely connected.

B. The form of this outline:
1. At some points, guidance will be taken, or precedents will be found, in certain traditional Anabaptist or Mennonite concepts.
2. The major headings of this supplement to the "theological statements" will be borrowed from the prior outline.

C. Since faith sees God as working in history to call into being a believing people:
1. We should not be attached to any definition of the "nature" of the human person as being static, but should welcome those views of man's nature which see him as growing, as changing, as produced by his history (and as producing his history). These changing views of man's nature are interpreted in light of the biblical position that man is morally inadequate, even rebellious.

2. God's saving purpose for the individual should not be limited to the "imputing" of a saved "status"; it must also be conceived as a call into a process, and experience, a growth, a social involvement.

3. The same must be said of lostness, which is not only a destiny of ultimate separation from God but also, already in this life, a process, a rebellion, a social involvement, and a pattern of leadings.

4. The young person is thus to be seen as bearing potentiality for learning in either direction. In line with the Anabaptist rejection of the traditional doctrine of original sin, which linked sinfulness to procreation, and which seemed to make God responsible for evil, the child should not be seen as evil, with a will which needs to be "broken" by education. In line with the Anabaptist rejection of infant baptism, the child should not be seen a young church member needing only to be sheltered from harmful influences. The human person is at all ages, in varying degrees, an arena where the awareness of self is born and cultivated in the context of choice between good and evil.

5. Apart from the call of God, man is in slavery to himself and to sin.

D. Since faith sees the church as a reconciled and reconciling community:

1. The individual must be understood as finding his true destiny not in heroic independence or autonomous self-fulfillment, but in self-forsaking, forgiving discovery of community, whose existence and whose mission are prior to his own.

E. Since membership is a matter of free "adult" decision:

1. No person may be assumed or presumed to be destined to membership. This is the meaning of the Anabaptist rejection of infant baptism.

2. The function of nurture in the believing family (and in its extension in formal schooling) is to enable, as much as possible, a responsible, mature, free, informed answer—be

it affirmative or negative—to the call of God, rather than to avoid such a choice or to predetermine that it shall necessarily be affirmative. A loving, faith-oriented environment may heighten the youth's awareness of Christians unerstandings, including the concept of his being a sinner and of Christ's forgiveness; but it may also heighten his knowledge of the demands of discipleship and his capacity to ward off his community's pressures upon him. There should be no assumption that the believer's children *must* become believers.

3. No judgment should be assumed with regard to the spiritual status of the young person before his clearly having made such a choice. This is the validity (whatever may be the theoretical shortcomings) of the traditional Mennonite concept of an age of accountability, prior to which children are not to be considered condemned. The numerous religious and moral experiences of which younger persons are capable may be fostered and respected without seeking to identify them as the commitment of Christian faith.

4. There is no one who is not called to this discipleship. This is the abiding validity of the Anabaptist denial of the concept of limited atonement and of the Anabaptist insistence upon the missionary imperative. No concept of the duties of believers toward their own children may be permitted to modify the primacy of the call of all men. The children of believers are socially privileged in their access to the gospel; they are not theologically privileged either by corporate election or by baptismal regeneration.

5. Genuine human decision has about it elements of gradual and rapid change. Concern for the authenticity of the choice forbids prescribing any age level or any one experiential pattern of conversion. The validity of the request for baptism is found not in a particular sequence of emotional experiences but in a set of understandings and a direction of commitment. It should be followed by further growth in knowledge, self-knowledge, and commitment, which again may proceed both gradually and in new crisis experiences.

6. Man may choose to identify by faith with Christ and the church.³

F. Since the disciples forsakes other values to follow Jesus Christ:

1. The person who is ready for the decision to follow Christ is one who has some experiential awareness of the other claims upon his loyalty: "the world, the flesh, and the devil."

2. The nurture of the children of believers should include a portrayal of those competing claims in their true light, but should not seek to "shield" the young person from the awareness of their attractiveness.

3. Compliance with the call of discipleship is voluntary. The ethic of suffering servanthood can be imposed on no one. Genuine commitment to Christ cannot be "programmed." Respect for the reticence of the uncommitted is part of the love in which the call is proclaimed and a recognition of the danger of an inauthentic response.

G. Since the disciple confesses in Jesus Christ the model of true humanity to which all men are called:

1. The call to love God and neighbor is addressed to all men; it is not a "special Christian ethic" irrelevant to unbelieving men, which would be wrong to propose as a model to those who choose not to believe.

2. On the other hand, the call is not to "self-fulfillment" or personhood apart from Jesus Christ. Christians need to ward off the temptation to work with others (in family, school, or service agency) on the assumption that full, normal, decent human existence is a self-sufficient wholeness to which faith would be an optional additive.

3. Nothing constitutive stands in the way of obedience to this call. This is the meaning of the Anabaptist rejection of the idea that original sin renders true belief and obedience impossible. The human person is seen as by grace capable of good, his disobedience is at least partly his own responsibility, and his repentance in the power of the Holy Spirit must

---

3. He does not choose to be a sinner. He already is.

be his own choice. We reject any views of "person" which make him the helpless object of forces beyond any control or the object of human control.

4. The renunciation of self to which Jesus' disciples are called is ratified by the gift of the new selfhood: "he that loseth his life . . . shall find it." If Christians are embarrassed to call all men to that renunciation which is portrayed in the "hard words" of Jesus, they betray their own unbelief in his promise. If they do not believe that the "strait and narrow way" is a gift of grace, that the call to "come and die" is a call to victory, they thereby reduce the gospel to a religiopsychlogical technique of self-starvation, and transform their own ethical earnestness into self-justification.

PART II

Articles from
CONCERN 13

4

Church and Mennonite College
Some Comments on the Relationships Between Two Communities

ALBERT J. MEYER AND WALTER KLAASSEN

The Church's Mandate in the Words of Christ

One common approach to an understanding of the church—we might almost call it the "textbook approach"—is to say that the church is characterized by (1) worship, (2) teaching, (3) fellowship, and (4) extension or mission. This approach has some value, but it certainly has limitations. The problem is that these four categories happen to represent the organization of the typical American Protestant congregation. There is a very serious temptation to reason in a circle. "The work of the church is doing what our congregation is doing." We tend to define "worship" as what our worship committee plans, "teaching" as what our Christian education department does, and to end where we started. It would be as if we were to say that a college was an institution characterized by concerns in academic affairs, student affairs, development, and finance—this hardly penetrates to the center of the matter, what actually happens when the students and teachers get together. In the case of the church, too, we are more likely to get to the heart of the matter if we begin with categories somewhat more remote from our immediate situations than the names of our church departments.

The early Anabaptists and some modern scholars have noticed clear and repeated mandates for the performing of four special functions in the church in the words of Jesus. They and we would suggest that these can be taken as a functional definition of the church. Each of these functions was especially prominent in the work of the New Testament church. From the emphasis on and repetition of the "words of Christ" in the Gospels authorizing the believers to function in these ways, it is evident that the early church felt that these functions were particularly important and that its authorization for performing these important tasks in God's name needed to be preserved for future generations. These particular "words of Christ" constituted the mandate of the Founder of the church to His followers.[1]

Sharing

The New Testament word is *koinonia* and it is most adequately translated as fellowship or communion. Again, since the word fellowship has today become more or less synonymous with service club conviviality, since communion has come in many quarters to refer specifically to the Lord's Supper, and since the Greek word *koinonia* has unfortunately become a slogan, we will use the word "sharing" and take it to mean everything that *koinonia* means. Hauck says that although *koinonia* means *Gemeinschaft* it also means participation or sharing.[2] C. T. Craig says that sharing is a more accurate translation of *koinonia* than fellowship.[3] This includes both the vertical and the horizontal according to 1 John 1:3: "So that you may have fellowship [*koinonia*] with us; and our fellowship [*koinonia*] is with the Father and with his Son Jesus Christ."

The mandate of Jesus to share comes to the church in His command to observe the Lord's Supper (1 Cor 11:23–26). But the Lord's Supper by itself does not exhaust the scope of the mandate. The Lord's

---

1. "Understanding the Church," No. 1–4, unpublished manuscript, Goshen, IN: 1958–59.

2. Gerhard Kittel, *Theologisches Wörterbuch zum Neuen Testament*, Vol. III (Stuttgart: Kohlhammer, 1960) 798.

3. C. T. Craig in The Beginnings of Christianity (New York: Abingdon, 1953) 133.

Supper is the expression in worship of the reality of sharing in the total life of the church. As Bonhoeffer says: "Fellowship . . . finds its goal and completion in the Lord's Supper."[4]

The compelling conviction of the earliest church about this mandate of Jesus can be felt in the words of Luke in Acts 2:42 and 4:32: "And they devoted themselves to the apostles' teaching and fellowship, to the breaking of bread and the prayers." "Now the company of those who believed were of one heart and soul, and no one said that any of the things which he possessed was his own, but they had everything in common." They shared first of all in the Holy Spirit that forged the company of believers into a body that was "of one heart and soul." "They were united by joy and gladness and a spirit of love that knew no bounds. It did not stop until it included sharing in material as well as spiritual goods."[5] The members were unconditionally committed to assist each other at every level of their existence. They were one because Christ is one.

Paul powerfully sets forth his convictions about sharing in 1 Corinthains 11. He argues on the basis of what he "received from the Lord" and what he had delivered to them when he first founded the church in Corinth. In the Corinthian church, sharing had broken down because of class-consciousness among the members, and this was reflected in the complete travesty that the Lord's Supper had become. The Supper was the objective demonstration of the unity of the believing body with its Lord. The proclamation of the Lord's death was not the sorrowful black crepe memorial service it so often is today, for in the earliest church "they broke bread with gladness." It was the celebration of the victory of the cross that had brought people, who had been separated by sin, together into a community of love. It was the feast of the anticipation of the final triumph of God over all opposition of His rule. It was also the objectivizing in worship of the unity of the church. Paul's censure of the Corinthians is not primarily that they have eaten or drunk too much, but that they have not "discerned the body," that they have "despised the church of God." The one loaf clearly signifies the one body (1 Cor 10:17). The very receiving of the bread and the wine is "participation in the body of Christ" (1 Cor 10:16). Sharing,

---

4 Dietrich Bonhoeffer, *The Cost of Discipleship* (London: SCM, 1959) 229.

5. Clarence T. Craig, *The Beginnings of Christianity* (New York: Abingdon, 1953) 141.

then, has to do with the unity of the body of Christ—the deepest fellowship and unity of men with each other and with God.

Binding and Loosing

These words are the New Testament terms for what has come to be known as church discipline. Basically, it refers to the making of decisions in ethical matters. The word discipline in this context, however, has for most people a negative value, hence our use of the New Testament terms. Moreover, the Anabaptists of the sixteenth century also used the biblical words frequently subsumed in the term "the rule of Christ." Christ Himself committed to the church the authority to forgive and retain sins, to bind and to loose. The best-known passage is Matt 18:15–20. The best textual evidence suggests that the words "against you" were not originally part of the text. It therefore reads simply, "If your brother sins, go and tell him his fault . . ." The implication of this is that the passage deals with any kind of sin in the church, not merely with personal affront. This divine mandate recognizes the presence of sin in the church and is the commission to deal with it redemptively. It means that the members of the church assume responsibility for each other, and that each one recognizes the voice of the brother as he is led by the Spirit as binding. This passage is not to be construed as a mandate to a hierarehy to bind and loose by virtue of sacramental ordination, nor as the collective opinion of the church against one of its members. This Matthew passage and John 20:22, 23 indicate that binding and loosing takes place only when Christ in His Spirit is present in the church. The presence of the Spirit ensures that what is dealt with is in fact sin and not merely cultural conformity. The presence of the Holy Spirit also means that the decision reached on earth in the church is honored in heaven. The presence of the Spirit gives the word of the church its binding and loosing quality.

The power of the keys is conferred on all the disciples, and each one assumes the responsibility. If a brother sins, another brother speaks to him. If he listens and repents both binding and loosing have taken place in that the erring brother was bound by the brotherly admonition to repent, and in that as he repented he was loosed of his sin. If he does not listen, others are brought in until at last, if necessary, the whole church is called on to deal with the matter. If repentance follows he is loosed from his sin by the church; if he persists in sin he has thereby excluded himself from the church and the church confirms it by regarding him as one who does not desire to obey Christ and can therefore not remain in the church.

Matthew 18:21–35, which follows immediately upon the binding and loosing passage, clearly implies that such disciplinary action is redemptive because there is no limit to forgiveness. A quotation from Karl Barth speaks to the importance of binding speech in the church.

> Can there and may there be in the Church speech which is not binding? Would it be a witness and confession if I did not thereby make the "unreasonable demand" of the other that he agree with me? Would we do one another honor by dispensing with this "unreasonable" and limiting ourselves to pure expressions of our own personal opinions? What have we to say to one another if we do not dare to speak bindingly with each other? Is not the very fact that so wretchedly little binding address is heard in the Church accountable for a goodly share of her misery—is it not perhaps the misery? Binding and loosing has to do with the integrity of the church.[6]

Discipling

The word comes from the great commission in Matt 28:19 where the command of Jesus is to "make disciples." It is the mandate for missionary preaching and baptism. In keeping with God's eternal purpose that mankind should become one body united in the love of God, Jesus' commission is to "make disciples of all nations." Everyone on earth must be told the good news. Those who hear and respond are to be baptized.

In baptism there is a twofold activity. First baptism is into Jesus Christ (Matt 28:19; Rom 6:3; Gal 3:27). That means that in baptism Christ appropriates that person for himself. He has been taken from the old creation and made a part of the new. This is, however, not the completely passive process that paedobaptists tend to make it. Romans 6 can hardly mean anything if it does not mean that the person who

---

6. Karl Barth, *The Church and the Political Problem of Our Day* (New York: Scribners, 1939) 82–83. Cited in Franklin H. Littell, *The Free Church* (Boston: Starr King, 1957) 113.

is baptized is aware of what is involved and that the memory of it "can always guide him in his attitude towards sin."[7]

In baptism he has died to the rule of sin and has been made over to Christ. He puts on Christ and begins a life which is growing into "the measure of the stature of the fullness of Christ." All of this is possible only if the individual is free to respond to the Word of grace. "Commitment to Christ in baptism is absolute and total."[8] All other loyalties receive their value by this one. The faith which God has given issues in unquestioning obedience to Christ the Lord of lords. Only such a person rightfully belongs to the church, for to Israel old and new it was said, "You shall be holy; for I . . . am holy" (Lev 19:2; 1 Pet 1:16), and thus holiness consists not merely of a ritual set-aside-ness without moral implications. This is clear from the Holiness Code (Lev 19:26) where holiness is made equivalent to being faithful to the neighbor, and also from 1 Pet 1:15 where holiness is enjoined in "conduct" (see also ethical injunctions in Paul's letters). Only the person who has deliberately and freely chosen Christ can obey and be holy in conduct.

Serving

The New Testament words are *diakonia* (service) and also to some extent the concept of *douleia* (slavery). Christ's mandate to His church to be a servant has more extensive synoptic support than any of the three foregoing functions. In this case it is a matter of limiting ourselves to several of the basic passages in which Jesus described His own vocation of suffering service, as well of that of the church, using terms drawn from Isaiah. Jesus Himself is the servant. In the synagogue at Nazareth He defined His vocation on behalf of others by using a quotation from Isaiah 61:

> The Spirit of the Lord is upon me,
> because he has anointed me to preach good news to the poor.
> He has sent me to proclaim release to the captives
> and recovering of sight to the blind,
> to set at liberty those who are oppressed,
> to proclaim the acceptable year of the Lord. (Luke 4:18–19)

7. William Klaassen, "Some Neglected Aspects in the Biblical View of the Church," *Concern*, 8 (1960) 3.

8. Ibid., 4.

Two further clear passages are found in Mark: "For the Son of man also came not to be served but to serve, and to give his life as a ransom for many." "This is my blood of the covenant, which is poured out for many" (Mark 10:45; 14:24). His service on behalf of others as spelled out in the Isaiah passage knows no limits; he goes on to give even his life in the service of others. (See also Luke 22:27.)

Paul's great words in Phil 2:7–8 express the same view. It is widely accepted as probable that the whole passage, verses 5–11, is in fact an early Christian hymn quoted by Paul and that it represents a very early view of the vocation of Jesus.[9] In Romans 15:8, Paul says that Christ "became a servant to Israel" (NEB).

Jesus Himself gave the mandate to service repeatedly, usually deriving it from His own vocation. "Whoever would be great among you must be your servant [*diakonos*], and whoever would be first among you must be slave [*doulos*] of all. For the Son of man also came not to be served but to serve [*diakonesai*] and to give his life as a ransom for many" (Mark 10:43–45; see also Mark 9:33–37; Luke 14:7–11; Matt 23:10–12). The derivation of the church's vocation of service from that of Jesus recurs in all the main blocks of New Testament literature. Paul clearly appeals to the example of Christ in Philippians 2 and 2 Cor 8:7–9. (See also Eph 4:20; Col 3:16.) One of the best-known supporting passages in this connection is 1 Pet 2:21–24. Christ is called the example of Christians. They have been called to the same suffering service which He freely rendered (see also Heb 12:2–3 and 13:15–16). The best statement is unquestionably found in John 13. Here, at the Last Supper, Jesus dons the attire of the slave and performs a slave's service. After he has finished he says to His disciples. "Do you know what I have done to you? You call me Teacher and Lord, and you are right, for so I am. If I then, your Lord and Teacher, have washed your feet, you ought also to wash one another's feet. For I have given you an example, that you also should do as I have done to you" (13:12–15). So strong is the servant motif here that one can hardly avoid the conviction that John has before him both Isaiah 42–53 and Philippians 2. Unassuming, humble service is the mandate. As the word *diakonia* is used for the lowly, unconditional service of Jesus, so it is used also for the vocation of His church. Paul in 2 Cor 5:18 writes about the service (*diakonia*) of reconciliation that

---

9. A. T. Hanson, *The Church of the Servant* (London: SCM, 1962) 40.

has been given us by God. Again it flows immediately out of Christ's reconciling service on the cross.

The specifics of the church's service are those of Christ's service as stated in the passage from Luke quoted above. The eschatological vision of Matt 25:35–36 mentions feeding the hungry and giving drink to the thirsty, taking care of the sick, having compassion on the stranger and visiting those in prison. Matt 5:38–42 enjoins disciples to refrain from insisting on their rights and to walk the second mile when necessary. Verses 43 and 44 require the Christian to love his enemy. Paul in Romans 12 expands that to looking after the physical needs of the enemy, instead of fighting him. Striving for peace is a service repeatedly enjoined in the New Testament.

Service, sharing, binding and loosing, and discipling are the mission of the church. Unless we properly emphasize all four of these functions, our doctrine of the church will only partially correspond to the New Testament design and will in consequence be unfaithful to the Gospel; it may be impoverished to the point of ineffectiveness and impotence.

Sociological Forms Assumed by the Church

We have seen that the church exists where Christians function together in binding and loosing, sharing, discipling, and serving as authorized by their Lord and as they are led by the Holy Spirit. But before we can consider the church and the Mennonite college more specifically, we have to ask about the concrete sociological forms which groups of Christians take as they work together in these churchly ways.

The New Testament term "church" (*ekklesia*) is used in the New Testament in at least three different ways.[10] In the first place, the term is used to refer to the church universal, the whole people of God. Secondly, there are references to churches in given cities or regions, to the church in Jerusalem, or the church at Antioch. This usage would probably correspond most closely to our use of the term "church" in the sense of "congregation." Finally, the term "church" is also used in

---

10. Harold S. Bender, "The Usage of the Term 'Church' in the New Testament," *Gospel Herald* 51:1 (1958) 1, 2, 21. Bender's reasons for saying that *ekklesia* was used in the New Testament also to mean "denomination" are weak; this point is considered later in this text.

the New Testament to refer to smaller groups of Christians meeting in homes, "house churches" or "small groups." It has often been noted that the New Testament never uses the term *ekklesia* to refer to church buildings. The church is essentially a group of people, not a building.

Whether the New Testament term *ekklesia* could have been appropriately used to refer to "denomination" (as in "General Conference Mennonite Church") is unclear. There were Judaizers and Hellenists in the church at Jerusalem. There were at least three denominations at Corinth.[11] That there were divisions is clear. However, the term "church" was rarely if ever applied to a single denomination in a place in which several existed.

Applying the term "church" to a denomination tends to imply a limitation on the universality of the church. The term "church" could be used in the New Testament to refer collectively to the group of Christians at Jerusalem, because it referred to all of the Christians in that region. "Church" could refer to groups on the house-church level because it then referred to all Christian members of a smaller natural social unit. But referring to the denominations at Corinth as separate "churches" tended to imply that in the city of Corinth there was a church of Paul, another church of Peter, and another of Apollos, rather than one church of Christ. There could be one church at Jerusalem and another at Antioch because Antioch and Jerusalem were different natural social units. Normally, a "church" is an assembly of all of the Christians in a natural social unit, not a special-interest group.

What are the natural social units in which churches would form today? Throughout most of the history of the church, local churches have formed on the basis of a geographical unit, the parish. In a modern city, however, there is a question as to whether the natural communities that exist are really primarily geographical. In specific situations, the most natural social units are vocational, intellectual, or even ethnic. (Even a superficial study of the social origins of American churches shows that most of our denominations have arisen from social or ethnic communities that were not geographically distinct one from another. European denominations are strikingly different in this regard.)

It would seem clear to the authors that to assume in the middle of the twentieth century that only geographical communities can be nat-

---

11. John Howard Yoder, "The Ecumenical Movement and the Faithful Church," *Focal Pamphlet Series*, No. 3 (Scottdale: Mennonite Publishing House, 1958) 19–24.

ural communities is unduly restrictive. Instead, a group of Christians brought together initially in the context of a given vocational, social, or even ethnic community could, if it agreed to assemble in the name of Christ and to function in the churchly ways described earlier in this paper, call itself a church. A group of Christians would not have to include the proportionate number of representatives of each race, class, and color found in the world, the United States, a state, or a county, to call itself a church. A group of Russian Mennonites can start a congregation, a group of students can form a small church. But such groups of Christians can properly call themselves churches only if they are actively engaged in discipling, that is, in communicating the gospel and bringing outside members into their groups. A group of Russian Mennonite Christians can form a congregation, but there is something wrong if there are only Russian Mennonite Christians in the congregation after years have passed.

If a denomination can be called a church, then, we would insist that modern Christians should normally function in the church on at least four levels: (1) church universal, (2) denomination-church, (3) congregational-church, and (4) small-group-church. The congregational-church and small-group-church levels are particularly important. A Christian cannot live a full Christian life by participating only in the church universal and ignoring life in a specific local congregation. A Christian can be a member of the General Conference Mennonite church, a denomination, only by being a member of a local congregation within that denomination. Discipling people in other lands (i.e., engaging in foreign mission work) is a function of the church that cannot be best exercised on the small-group-church level, or even on the congregational-church level. On the other hand, it is almost impossible for a congregational-church of five hundred or a thousand members to consider adequately and in context even the most important ethical decisions of its members. How can a congregational-church of five hundred give much help in plenary sessions to the vocational decision-making of its young people without resorting to the kinds of generalities that often do as much harm as good? Binding and loosing in such situations is almost certain to be legalistic. Where small-group-church, subcongregational units, do not exist, members do not ordinarily feel much of a sense of responsibility for binding and loosing; this aspect of Christ's commission to his church is simply ignored.

Christians may engage in one of the functions of the church, such as discipling, more on one or two of the levels on which they participate in the church than on others. Their activities on the various levels on which the church exists will not compete with their activities on other levels. Their activities in the small-group church will complement rather than duplicate their activities as members of the denomination. Membership in a congregation does not interfere with a Christian's membership in his denomination; in fact, it is usually his only way of being a member of the denomination. Membership in a small-group church should further rather than interfere with the Christian's membership in his congregation—our existing Sunday school classes, which meet some of the needs on the small-group church level at present, even though they have seen their task as primarily educational, have certainly stimulated spiritual life in our congregations. Problems can arise, of course. For example, a congregation can find itself at variance with the majority of the other congregations in the denomination. A Christian in such a congregation can find that tension between his loyalty to his congregation and his loyalty to his denomination. But such situations are not normal. Ordinarily, an individual's loyalty to his congregation is a means of expressing his loyalty to his denomination. Ordinarily, the church will take form on all of the four levels we have been discussing if it is really the church.

A concluding comment on the sizes of congregations and small-group churches may be appropriate. The fact that members of a congregation participate also in small-group churches within the congregation does not mean that the size of the congregation is unimportant. What we have said about small-group churches certainly does not imply that a congregation should be as small as possible. Optimum sizes of congregations and small-group churches depend on the churchly functions conducted on each level.

Social psychologists have pointed out that the formation and functioning of subgroups of a larger social unit of congregational size are inhibited when, on one hand, the larger group becomes so large that the members form a mass rather than a real social group or when, on the other, the larger group becomes so small that it begins to function like a small-group-church itself.[12] The limits, especially the upper

12. Theodore M. Newcomb, "Student Peer-Group Influence. In *Personality Factors on the College Campus*, edited by Robert L. Sutherland et al. (Austin, TX: Hogg

limit, obviously, depend partly on the mobility of the population of which the larger group is composed. The large group should be small enough that almost all of the members know each other by name. For groups of the mobility of average Mennonite church members, an upper limit would probably be between 300 and 600. A minister could preach to 2,000 or 3,000 members as well as to 400, but a congregation in the Mennonite understanding is not a mass of people listening to one preacher or related to each other primarily through one man.[13] On the other hand, we would see no point in a strategy of forming congregations of less than 100 or 150 members in areas of large Mennonite populations. Such congregations cannot function as small-group churches in any case—the maximum number of members in a small-group-church should be twenty or less—and the fact that the whole congregation is small may actually interfere with the proper functioning of the small-group-churches within the congregation.

The authors recognize the tentative character of some of the assertions in the preceding paragraphs. The mobility of Mennonite populations varies widely. In given situations, other factors may be much more important than the size-of-congregation factor in inhibiting or promoting the formation of small-group churches. Social scientists are not themselves agreed on the importance of the size-of-group factor. From our own experience, however, we would suggest that Mennonites should think more carefully about the sizes most appropriate to the various forms the church takes in local situations in the future than they have in the past.[14]

Foundation for Mental Health, 1962) 81. Newcomb did the classic study of students at Bennington College in the 1930s.

13. Some congregations have tried to solve growth problems by holding two parallel Sunday morning services. This arrangement does not seem to us to provide a basic solution—neither of the groups meeting in this way is a congregation, and the congregation itself may never congregate at all. This is hardly full church functioning on the congregational level . . . In some such circumstances, it might be better if the congregation would divide into two congregations, each of which would meet while the other had Sunday school.

14. It is interesting to note that this question has received a little thought in some circles. The average size of (old) Mennonite congregations has decreased, in the past ten or fifteen years, because of an emphasis in some areas on dividing very large congregations into smaller congregations and mission centers.

The Church and the Mennonite College

We come now to speak specifically about the Mennonite college on the basis of the foregoing analysis.

The Sponsoring Denomination

Mennonite colleges are regarded as institutions designed primarily to serve the educational needs of Mennonite constituencies and secondarily also of the broader non-Mennonite communities surrounding the colleges. No existing Mennonite colleges require that students must be Christian to be admitted as students; the conditions for admission are primarily academic and social. This means that, on each campus, both Christian and non-Christian students comprise the college community. On biblical and historical grounds, we cannot, therefore, consider the whole college community as such to be the church. The church-related college is established and supported by the church but academic community and spiritual community are not coextensive.

The community of faith, the church, is responsible to God in its relationships with the community of learning just as it is responsible to God in its relationships with every other human community. Because the Christian college or university is a place at which Christ and culture confront each other most intensely, the church must be wide-awake to its responsibility in that place. In *Faith and Learning*, Alexander Miller says:

> The church owes to the university the best of the Christian heritage with all the illumination it provides upon the structure and meaning of human existence and in particular of intellectual life and responsibility. The church owes it; but it does not always provide it. But now the church for its very life on the campus, to generate and nurture the kind of lay witness on which the Christian enterprise will crucially depend, must seek out the sources of its own generation and regeneration. By the same token, by drawing deep from the Biblical and classical faith which is the gift of God to His people, it will best serve an academic community which for the repairing of its own structure and the correction of its own vision needs precisely the help of those resources which are not humanly contrived but divinely gifted.[15]

15. Alexander Miller, *Faith and Learning: Christian Faith and Higher Education in Twentieth Century America* (New York: Association Press, 1960) 154.

Academic Community and Spiritual Community

At a Mennonite college, students should expect to receive (1) a solid small-college liberal arts education, (2) an intensive experience in spiritual community, and (3) substantial studies in Bible, Christian thought, church history, and the relevance of the Christian faith for the various academic disciplines. Students attend college first of all to learn—not just to go to church. But the spiritual experiences in college life are very properly of concern to faculty members and students. They are also learning experiences. Just as laboratory and lecture sessions are both integral parts of most science courses, so co-curricular and curricular experiences in the Christian faith are integral parts of the total college experience of Christian students. The academic community, as an academic community, can appropriately call each of its members to consider all important aspects of human experience, including the history and relevance of the Christian faith, before proceeding to build his personal philosophy of life.

If this were all there were to the matter, academic community and spiritual community could be one. The problem is not that God has created a world in which Christ and culture are necessarily in conflict. The problem is rather that, in God's world, some people—people who are also culture-producers—have chosen to have nothing to do with Christ. Sin and evil exist. They may not be logical or rational in God's world, but they nevertheless exist—and any approach to human existence that does not take them into account is not dealing with the real world. The academic and spiritual aspects of the church-college experience can form a single, integrated whole—but the problem is that some students do not want the whole experience.

The analysis of the life of Christians in the academic community, just as the analysis of the life of the church in the larger human society, must take these facts into account.[16]

Human communities ordinarily have certain sets of expectations or standards applicable to their members. Colleges are no exception. We may refer to the set of expectations and standards of a given college as

---

16. In what follows, we focus our attention primarily on the relevance of a Mennonite understanding of spiritual community for the structuring of religious life on a Mennonite college campus. Our understanding of the church may also have implications for the structures of our academic communities, however. This is discussed briefly in Appendix 3.

its discipline. When we consider the kinds of disciplines appropriate to colleges in which there are overlapping spiritual and academic communities, four possible options present themselves. The first three of these are in use in most American and Canadian colleges and universities.

1. Accept only Christians as students and provide a uniform academic, social, and religious discipline for all. (This option is characteristic of some Bible institutes and the colleges of certain denominations.)
2. Accept Christians and non-Christians and subject all to a uniform academic, social, and religious discipline. (This is approximately what obtains at present at Bethel College and most other Christian colleges.)
3. Accept Christians and non-Christians and have academic, a minimum of social, but no religious discipline. (This obtains at most state-supported and at many private colleges and universities.)
4. Accept Christians and non-Christians and provide a minimum academic and social discipline which students either accept or reject depending on whether they wish to be associated with the Christian church or not.

In order to reach our goals in our work with both the Christian and the non-Christian students in our Mennonite liberal arts colleges, and on the basis of the biblical and Mennonite traditions we exist to represent, we have no choice but to choose the last of the four listed alternatives. In situations in which a spiritual community and other communities overlap—and we have already discussed the existence of overlapping academic and spiritual communities on our church-college campuses—all of the other options violate the biblical and Mennonite view of the church and its relationship to the world. The reasons for this will be spelled out in what follows.

Freedom of Decision

Freedom of decision is called for by both the Western academic tradition and the Christian church. The proper functioning of *academe* is impossible unless her members can make hypotheses and explore their implications freely. The Bible assumes from beginning to end that man is free to make responsible choices, an emphasis especially marked in the Anabaptist movement of the sixteenth century, in contrast to

Roman Catholic, Lutheran, and Reformed Christianity. *Ekklesia* cannot be *ekklesia* unless people are free to decide whether or not they want to belong to her and to live their lives within her.

The time that students spend in college is not a parenthesis. Calls to decision are not just waived for that period of time. It is a strange misphrasing of his case that led John Dillenberger in his essay, "A Protestant Understanding of Church and University," to imply that it is wrong to want people to be totally committed in the university because of the need for examining life at leisure.[17] Time spent at college is part of life and we are in no position to rule that this time is exempt from making religious decisions; it is God, not man, who calls for decision. In fact, one could argue that religious decisions are especially important at college, because other life decisions like choosing a mate and an occupation require clear religious convictions if they are to be made meaningfully.

In a Christian college the gospel is proclaimed as in any other social structure, and persons in the academic community are called upon to decide either for or against it. To provide the freedom called for in both *academe* and *ekklesia*, we propose the following as a way in which the options might be stated.

Option A. This option involves the acceptance of minimum required rules of order in the academic and social spheres, in order to establish and maintain an appropriate academic tradition and a reasonably orderly social life. It would include certain courses in Bible and church history necessary to an understanding of Western culture.[18] Because the college as an academic community would want all of its members to consider all important aspects of human experience in building their personal philosophies of life, it would also include certain lectures and convocations in which the Christian way of life would be presented, possibly among alternatives, as a live option. The minimum standards of Option A would be required of all students in the college.

17. *The Mission of the Christian College in the Modern World.* Addresses and Reports of the Third Quadrennial Convocation of Christian Colleges, 1962, St. Olaf College, Northfield, Minn, 48.

18. It is simply a fact that much in Western culture cannot be properly appreciated and understood without knowledge of its Christian roots. For example, George Buttrick says that "students should know the Biblical faith which, like a wise home, nourished the scientific learning of our western world" (*Biblical Thought and the Secular University*, Baton Rouge: Louisiana State University Press, 1960, 13).

Option B. This discipline is an option set by the spiritual community on campus, not by the entire academic community. It would include the requirement of attendance at chapel, Sunday worship services, and at small-group-church discussion, Bible study, prayer and service meetings on Sundays or during the week. Violations of the standards of the Christian community on campus would be treated not as student personnel or office problems, but as problems in the community of those who had made Christian commitments to one another.

Christians are ordinarily willing to identify themselves—this is a rather minimal form of witnessing. It is not at all unreasonable to ask students who seek to live as Christians on the campus to indicate this and to show some interest in participating in the various forms the church takes on campus. For freshmen, the question might be posed after certain required explanatory chapel services (or freshmen orientation sessions) in the fall. Or it could be raised in private sessions each new student would have with an older student or faculty member. Although faculty members and administrators might indicate that the availability of Option B was one of the reasons for the existence of the college, they would not in any way discriminate against students choosing Option A. Moreover, Option B would remain open to students at all times. Naturally, there would be a concern on the part of the community of faith to persuade students to become Christians and to accept the disciplines of Option B. The very existence of the two options would remind students of the fact that Christian students and faculty members were not primarily interested in getting students to behave themselves in the dormitories, but rather in having them voluntarily and freely choose to live in Christ.

Naturally there might he some students who would be members of Mennonite congregations who would not wish to elect Option B. Christians of some other denominations might consciously and clearly reject our concept of the church. Since the spiritual community in a Mennonite college would be affiliated with the Mennonite Church, and since we believe that we have a contribution to make to ecumenical discussion precisely at the point of the nature of the church, discussions with Christians of other denominations might well ensue. Problems of these kinds would require careful handling, and, presumably, the cooperation of the pastor of the home congregation and students and faculty members on the campus in the attempt to reach clear understandings. These discussions would be worthwhile in their own right.¹⁹ In any case, Mennonite students who are not interested in working with the church on campus would not be ignored or patted on the back and told they would grow out of adolescence.

Division: An Inevitable Consequence of Freedom of Decision

The biblical doctrine of the church rediscovered by our forefathers in the sixteenth century speaks of a clear separation of church and world. This means primarily that each young person must be faced clearly and decisively with the claims of the gospel and discipleship and be accorded the freedom, as much as humanly possible, from all pressure to make a choice either for or against Christ. We can no longer continue our thinly disguised *Volkskirche* in which young people find it so hard to come to a truly personal, and therefore, meaningful, decision. For the sake of the young people the overly protective and fearful attitude which does not trust them with vital decisions must be abandoned. It cannot be maintained if we wish to be biblical Mennonite Christians. We must face and accept the risk that some students will take us at our word and choose Option A with all of the consequences. There will likely be Mennonite students taking this course who have, by parents, home church, and pastor, been considered loyal members of the church. Such an event would, however, not be irremediably evil, since then both student and college would know the truth and the claims of the gospel could be brought to the student in an atmosphere cleared of confusion. It would be much healthier to have a student say "no" to the Christian faith honestly than to chafe constantly under a discipline that had no meaning for him. The words of Conrad Grebel may sound quaint, but the point they make is as relevant today as it has ever been:

> It is much better that a few be rightly taught through the Word of God, believing and walking aright in virtues and practices,

---

19. It should be noted that almost any social—not necessarily religious—college discipline leads to questions in some cases. For example, the children from families where alcoholic beverages are used may wonder why the college has rules on drinking. Our assertion here is that the existence of the proposed structures would help to keep the questions that are raised phrased in terms of the basic issues as Mennonites understand them.

than that many believe falsely and deceitfully through adulterated doctrine.[20]

One of the functions of a Christian college is to confront all its members with the call of God in the context of choice. This must be done.

We must face and accept the risk of a clear division between church and world within the college. That church and world exist side by side even in a Christian college needs no elaboration. What needs emphasis is that the lines between them be drawn so that they can be seen. To be light, the church must be visible.

> Do not think that I have come to bring peace on earth; I have not come to bring peace, but a sword. For I have come to set a man against his father . . . and a man's foes will be those of his own household. He who loves father or mother more than me is not worthy of me. . . . He who finds his life will lose it, and he who loses his life for my sake will find it. (Matt 10:34–39)

Response to the call of Christ will, if clearly and decisively made, lead to division among men, for there are those who reject it. The life of discipleship to which Christ calls men is so radical that those who accept it and live it will be set off from their fellows. The divisions will come precisely at the point of the closest human relationships, in the family and where people live together. We cannot escape the imperative of this word of Jesus.

Finally, we must face and accept the risk of exposing the church to the world. The words of Jesus especially lay upon Christians the responsibility for self-exposure in order to make a meaningful witness appropriate to a given situation. "I send you forth as sheep among wolves" (Matt 10:16)—the absolute defenselessness of sheep illustrates the radical requirement of exposure. Matthew 10:34–39 also clearly implies that measures designed to protect us from exposure, however hallowed they may be in custom, are a denial of Christ. "You are the light of the world." A light exposes itself to the darkness and also the danger of being blown out. We remember here the little oil lamps with the open flame used in Jesus' day. "You are the salt of the earth." Salt is not kept in a salt sack; it is used. Nor is it put in a watertight container in the soup but right into the soup where it dissolves. It is exposed to

---

20. [See Hans J. Hillerbrand, *The Protestant Reformation* (New York: Harper & Row, 1964) 126. —Ed.]

dissolution. In both the case of the light and salt, Jesus does not say, "You have light and salt" but "You *are* light and salt."[21] We can in no way escape from exposure if we will be true to the imperative of discipleship. We cannot witness to the world unless we say, "We face the same temptations as you do. We too live in the need of God's love and forgiveness."

In other words, the nature of the "separation" of church and world must be clearly understood. Basically, it is inextricably bound up with the Mennonite beliefs in freedom of decision and adult baptism. The church is defined by its "yes" to Christ. "World," in our present usage of the term, refers to men in societies who have not said this "yes" to Christ. The church lives and works in the world, but there is a distinction between church and world, because a decision men must make when they face Christ is a real one. People answer the all-important question in different ways, and there is inevitable division.

Congregational-Church Life on the Mennonite College Campus

In previous sections of this paper, we have seen that the church exists where Christians live and work together as authorized by Jesus Christ and as they are led by the Holy Spirit. We have seen that the church exists on various levels, and that one of these is the congregational-church level. In the present section, we ask about the concrete forms congregational-church life will take on the Mennonite college campus.

One of the starting points from which we wish to begin in this section is the assertion that, other things being equal, and on a given level of church functioning, a Christian should involve himself deeply in the life of one or two churches rather than to participate superficially in more. This principle is appropriate on the small-group church level, as well as on the congregational-church level, but we are here talking about the congregational-church level, in which Christians ordinarily assemble in groups of fifty members or more. Rather than to attend a different congregation each Sunday of the month, a Christian should normally seek to involve himself deeply in the life of one, or at most two, congregations.

21. Bonhoeffer, *Cost of Discipleship*, 69.

Furthermore, a Christian will normally be able to sink his roots most deeply in the community in which he works during the week. In a sense, this is his "natural" community, a concept to which we referred earlier. In rural farming areas this is likely to be defined geographically; in urban areas, this is more likely to be defined vocationally. In any case, a Christian does not ordinarily attend a congregation to get acquainted with new people or for diversion. As he goes about the daily work to which God has called him in the weekday community or communities of which he is a part, his purpose is rather to seek association with his fellow Christians in those communities in order that God's new humanity may become visible and flourish in those places also. He will ordinarily be able to involve himself most deeply—in binding and loosing, in sharing, and so on—in a group that includes those Christians with whom he associates from time to time during the week.[22]

The problem of Mennonite college students—as well as of other mobile Mennonites—is clear. A Mennonite college student meets with his fellow Christians in groups of fifty or more members in at least three different contexts: (1) his home congregation, (2) the college congregation or a Mennonite congregation near the college, and (3) sessions of all members of the student Christian group on campus (e.g., the Student Christian Fellowship, Young People's Christian Association, or Student Christian Association). Almost all church colleges also provide for weekday chapel service for members of the campus community. These are usually viewed as worship services, although the extent to which the group that congregates for the services views itself as a worshiping congregation varies from campus to campus. Whether or not the chapel group can appropriately be called a congregation—church—it is certainly of congregational size—and whether or not what it does can appropriately be called worship depends on a number of considerations: whether or not non-Christians are required to attend, the degree to which members of the group participate in planning the

---

22. The situation of missionaries who are the first to enter new unchurched areas is not under discussion here. Until the nucleus of a new church is established, a missionary in such a situation normally has his deepest roots in the sending congregation. He is absent from the regular meetings of that congregation because of the very special nature of the work to which God has called him. When the nucleus of a new congregation forms, all of the above considerations apply.

services, the degree to which members are conscious of their mutual responsibilities, and worship in the full sense of the terms (in sharing, discipling, and serving, as well as in listening to prepared talks), and on the degree to which the chapel group is aware of its relationship to the whole church of Christ in its various forms. In any case (1) Mennonite college students often participate in congregational-church life in so many different contexts that they have no deep rooting in any congregations, and (2) they often participate in congregational-church life most superficially in the college community, the community in which they spend most of their time during the four years of their college experience and the social unit that could most logically be considered a student's "natural" community.

We believe that this statement of the problem can go a long way toward a solution. As Mennonites, we have been influenced too much by the typical church-college pattern we have found in the Protestant colleges around us. With Roman Catholic, Lutheran, and Reformed Christians, we have tended to assume that "religious experiences" are good for students in themselves, regardless of the forms of group life in which they occur and regardless of the attitudes of the participants. The "religious experiences" in congregation-sized units provided for students have not been sufficiently coordinated with one another; the result has often been that students have not been deeply involved in congregational life in any form.

We believe that resident students at a Mennonite college should normally involve themselves primarily in the life of one or two congregations at or near the campus. In some cases, a single college church, most of whose members would be students and faculty members who could meet for chapel services during the week and services on Sunday mornings, would be best. In this situation, it would have to be understood that some students and faculty members might worship in other congregations on Sunday mornings, and that the families of students and faculty members would not ordinarily be able to assemble with the congregation in the chapel services during the week. In many situations, there will probably have to be a greater compromise with the principle that students should involve themselves deeply in the life of a single congregation wherever possible. In such situations, the weekday chapel congregation and the Sunday church congregation will be organized as distinct congregations. This must be the case when the

Sunday congregation is a congregation at the college, rather than a college congregation. Even in this situation, the two congregations in which students participate can be very closely coordinated. Students can have responsibilities, including some leadership responsibilities, in each. They should involve themselves deeply in both.

In situations in which there are one or more congregations near the campus, the question as to whether or not a college congregation, a congregation composed primarily of faculty members and students and meeting on Sundays as well as weekdays, should be formed will have to be answered in the light of local circumstances. At Goshen and Bethel, congregations that begun as college congregations have increasingly moved in the direction of becoming congregations at, that is, geographically near, the college. The evolution of the congregations in this direction has probably been good, but the continuation of this evolution may at a certain point require that the following questions be raised: Is the non-college participation in the Sunday congregation so large that it becomes hard to coordinate the Sunday and the weekday congregations of the students? Do students have enough contacts with non-college members of the Sunday congregation to permit them to get personally acquainted with most of them in a reasonable period of time?[23]

The question has sometimes been raised as to whether students should not have a "normal" church life. The discussion of this hinges entirely, of course, on what one means by "normal." We have implied that a "normal" congregation in a rural farming community is such, not so much because all ages meet together on Sunday mornings, but because all of the people living in a certain natural community meet together and because each has his own responsibilities.

Asking young people to leave their own communities and to assemble in one place for study is abnormal in one sense—but it is precisely the way to create the kind of academic community that is so important in education. Much of what can be learned in college can be learned from books by a student living in his home community, but bringing students together to learn together and to stimulate each other in their studies in a situation somewhat removed from the more

---

23. These questions must also be raised, of course, when the enrollment in a church college itself becomes so large that members of the campus community cannot become personally acquainted with one another. We will not discuss this situation further here.

routine concerns of the workaday world is so clearly desirable that it hardly requires discussion. We do not apologize when an academic community does not contain people of all levels of interest in intellectual matters. Indeed, in order to make it possible for students to achieve their academic goals in the best way, we plan it this way.

Granted the initial abnormality in the population of a community composed almost entirely of church college students, what we are saying is that the most normal type of church life in this natural community, some of whose members have joined the community partly because of spiritual interests, would be a life in which the Christians in this community would meet as a congregation. There may be something enjoyable in a way about "shopping around" or about "sitting in" on a congregation without getting involved during the week, but there is nothing "normal" about superficial church life.

One of the bases of the students' choice between the two options discussed in the preceding sections would be his choice as to whether or not he wished to participate fully in the life of a congregational-church while he was in college. In a Mennonite residential college, students would normally participate in the campus congregation during the week and in either the campus congregation or a congregation near the campus on Sundays. A student close enough to his home to go home frequently might decide to return to the college congregation on Sunday mornings, even when he was otherwise at home on the weekend. (He might also go home each Sunday morning and participate actively in the life of his home congregation on Sundays, although that would seem to be somewhat less desirable because of the greater separation between his Sunday and his weekday congregational activities.) In any case, the important thing would be the student's involvement in depth in the life of the one or two congregations in which he chose to participate.

Small-Group-Churches on the Mennonite College Campus

We have already referred to the small-group church level of church functioning in an earlier section of this paper. In fact, we have noted that there are some aspects of the work of the church for which the small-group church level of functioning is necessary. In matters demanding knowledge of immediate circumstances of the situation, such as vocational decision-making, binding and loosing, if carried on at all by a large group are almost certain to become legalistic. Sharing occurs most freely among church members when they are rather intimately acquainted with one another. For many years writers and workers in the church have viewed the Sunday school, a limited form of small-group church life in the church, as an important element in the church's outreach. Or to cite another example, the Mennonite Central Committee has for years used small groups of workers in its service programs at home and abroad. Not all of these small groups would view themselves as small churches. The important point is that small groups can work in important ways in all four of the primary functions of the church outlined in earlier sections of this paper.

This is not to say that small-group churches can do all the church needs to do in sharing, binding and loosing, discipling, and serving. There are some important activities of the church that are most appropriately engaged in on the congregational and denominational levels. What we are rather asserting is that participating in the life of the church on both the small-group-church and congregational-church levels is not normally to be considered an optional matter for Christians—working on both levels is a necessary part of engaging in the full work of God's people.

The Small-Group Church Is a Church

Basically, this is to say that the small-group church should not view itself primarily as a special-interest group. If its members are primarily farmers, or primarily students, they may recognize the limitations in their range of interests—but they should do this in exactly the way in which a congregation composed of only white people in a world in which many people are not white—or a congregation of Mennonites in a Christian church in which most members are not Mennonite—will recognize the abnormalities in its situation. Recognizing their situations, all of these forms of the church should still seek to live faithfully under the guidance of the Holy Spirit as local manifestations of the church.

One of the problems of the Sunday school for adults in many churches has been that it has been viewed primarily as a school and that its purpose has been viewed as primarily educational. (This can be said, even though the adult Sunday school has not ordinarily included the elements of course evaluation and promotion to the study of new and more difficult subjects which are characteristic of almost all other educational institutions.) It is simply not evident that education is basically a small-group activity, and that prophecy—that is, preaching, explaining the relevance of God's Word to immediate and concrete situations in which particular people are living—is essentially a large-group activity. If God's Word is really to be made relevant to the specific situation in which one of the members of the church is living, is it not possible that the prophetic word the member needs might not just as appropriately be brought to him by one of his fellow Christians in a small group? Is it not true that the sermon has a very important educational, as well as prophetic, function in the life of the ordinary congregation? Indeed, some sermons tend to be more educational than prophetic. In any case, we would propose that neither congregation-churches nor small-group churches should be viewed as special-interest groups engaging in only one or two activities. We are rather proposing that congregational-church and small-group church should each engage in all of these aspects of the functions of the church appropriate to its level.

These comments apply immediately to small-group churches on the Mennonite college campus. Their purpose is not to engage in Bible study alone. They are not just discussion groups. They should include corporate prayer, service and action projects where appropriate, and fellowship opportunities, but they are not just prayer cells, action committees, or social groups. They should include all of these activities as they are led by the Spirit.[24] Their action projects should follow from their group studies and prayer concerns, and their outreach and service activities will ordinarily raise questions they will want to pursue further in study. It is not that they will do all of these things at once. It is rather that they will recognize the range of responsibilities they face as Christians and will move from step to step as the Holy Spirit leads them, without insisting that the pattern follow the special interests with which they may have come together initially.

---

24. Where orderly relationships and understandings with the larger congregation of which they are subgroups are maintained, small-group churches, as well as the larger congregation, may appropriately observe the Lord's Supper.

One point needs special attention. Discussion occurring in a small-group church meeting is not just discussion for its own sake. Members should be encouraged to express themselves. Sitting around tables or in a circle helps. Using a blackboard can help keep the foci of the discussion clear. Multiple leadership also helps—a speaker should not ordinarily be asked to lead the discussion on his own presentation. But the discussion does not exist for its own sake. There is in both college and church a passionate interest in the truth. Freshmen are not ordinarily asked in college classes for discussion and a majority vote on the question as to whether or not Paul went to Rome! Small-group members will show a similar concern for finding the best methods for use in their search for truth; they will not assume that everything can be done by discussion just because a small group does happen to permit discussions almost impossible in larger groups.

These observations are not particularly new.[25] In many churches, the liveliest Sunday-school classes have been those that have undertaken a wide range of group projects and activities; they have not engaged only in activities ordinarily considered "educational."

In an earlier section on congregational life, we said that deep involvement in the life of one congregation was better than superficial participation in several congregations. This is also the point here. Many church members and college students belong to a great number of discussion groups, prayer cells, action committees, etc. The point is not that these people should be doing more discussing, praying, or fellowshiping. The point is rather that they should meet with one small group which engages in several of these activities four times a month, rather than with four different special-interest groups holding monthly meetings. One of the goals of small-group church functioning in the congregation should be to reduce fragmentation and proliferation of activities in church life.

---

25. Some very practical comments on small groups in nonstudent congregations are given in Robert A. Raines, *New Life in the Church* (New York: Harper & Row, 1961), and Elizabeth O'Connor, *Call to Commitment* (New York: Harper & Row, 1963). More general observations were presented by Elton Trueblood at Bethel College in the 1960 Menno Simons Lectures; these have been published as *The Company of the Committed* (New York: Harper & Row, 1961). Marginal note: Raines comments (28) on the importance of conversions of middle-aged people.

2. Small-Group-Churches Require Appropriate Procedures and Structures[26]

Informal small-group-church meetings do not require fewer structures than formal small-group-church meetings; they require different structures. In one sense, a Sunday-school class with a teacher who lectures requires very little structure—whatever planning is done is done by one person. Our experience with small groups has shown the desirability of having more structure than this.

The Bethel College Student Christian Fellowship groups with which we have been associated have required that members commit themselves to regular attendance. The work of the church cannot be conducted haphazardly—it is certainly as important as the course work in which students engage during the week. Ordinarily, every participant signs a sheet passed around during the meeting. When a member indicates, through nonattendance or otherwise, that a group has not given adequate attention to certain subjects or concerns he has, a member of the small-group steering committee talks with him. This has been found to be a most useful way of helping "fringe" members come into the group and make their voices heard.

Each small group has had a steering committee. Experience has shown that continuing relevance in the discussions and projects is most easily maintained when several students from the group meet each week with the non-student participants. The committee decides who should open the next meeting with prayer, and possibly with an appropriate Scripture reading, whether to have a presentation, where to begin the discussion, if there is to be one, and, generally, how to spend the available group meeting time most profitably. When one of us has been asked to prepare a presentation for the meeting, the students have often heard and commented in advance on the outline of the presentation. The steering committee tries to plan for the presentations several weeks in advance and to be sensitive to the interests and feelings of the group members. On several occasions, several meetings were held

---

26. This section is based in part on notes sent by the Bethel College Student Christian Fellowship Executive Committee to leaders of student groups in the school year 1962–63. Kay Peters, David Schmidt, and Joanne Zerger were among the members of the Executive Committee. One of the authors worked with the Executive Committee as faculty sponsor; the committee consulted with both of the authors at times in the preparation of the sets of notes.

in one week, and the members of the steering committee divided up the names of the members of the group and saw each one personally between the steering committee sessions.

The student members of the steering committees have been elected by the small groups on one of the first Sundays of the school year. The following procedure has been found useful: On one Sunday each member of the group is asked to nominate a number of people equal to the number needed on the committee. If a committee of three members (the usual number) is desired, the names of the five or six with the highest number of votes are presented at the election on the next Sunday. Additional individual nominations can be received on the second Sunday to make sure all candidates are on the slate. This procedure permits time for careful nominations (the nomination ballots are distributed at the opening and collected at the end of the group meeting) and takes less actual group time than some alternate procedures. It encourages every member to express himself in the nomination, as well as in the election—this is often missing in nominations and elections in small groups and committees. In our groups, the nominations have normally followed an explanation of the purposes of the steering committee, a special set of readings from the Bible, and some remarks on the importance of recognizing and benefiting from members' gifts in the Christian church. These details are not always matters of small consequence. It is very important that elections in the church be selections of spiritual leaders rather than popularity contests. Informality in a small group is not carelessness or inattention to detail.

Faculty members and adults from the Newton area, as well as students, have been members of the small church groups at Bethel. Students have been very active in the leadership of the small groups; this does not imply that faculty members should stay in the background. In this case, as in the election of steering committee members, the guiding principle should be that gifts of the Spirit should be recognized and their use encouraged wherever they are found. Non-student participants should neither dominate nor abdicate all responsibility. As older and more experienced Christians, and as people with some leadership abilities and experiences in classroom and on campus, one would normally expect faculty small-group participants to have important contributions to make to the groups with which they meet. Their contributions will not always be the same: one will have special theological qualifications, while another will be an especially good discussion leader. Non-student participants will normally be able to bring ideas and a sense of continuity to steering committee meetings. The degree to which a non-student participant will play a given role in a small group will depend to some extent on the roles the student leaders are able to play. In any case, it should be in the interest of all group members that the gifts of the Spirit to students and non-students alike be recognized and exercised for the benefit of the whole group.

Our experience at Bethel indicates the importance of division when a group increases in size to more than about fifteen or twenty members. Partly as a consequence on an emphasis on witnessing on campus, members have invited Christian and non-Christian friends to join their small groups. More of this could have been done. A general invitation to all students has been issued at the opening of each quarter. During the quarter, new members are often asked to wait a week or two until a new subject is opened before starting to attend—the presence of visitors can interfere with a discussion based on the presentations and discussions of the previous weeks. In any case, the small church groups have frequently grown to the point where they have had to consider division.

Division never seems to look very inviting in prospect.[27] The procedure Bethel groups have ordinarily followed to make the transition as smooth as possible has been to ask each group member to put on a slip of paper his name and the names of about two other group members whom he would most like to have with him in his group after division. One of the members of the steering committee then privately constructs a sociogram and divides the group into two groups in such a way that there are the fewest number of persons separated from others they would like to be with. Lists of the names for each of the two groups are brought to the next meeting, and the two groups separate at that time. (Any student who feels strongly that he would not like to join the group to which he is assigned is invited to join the other group, but students have rarely taken this opportunity.) The whole procedure is less awkward when there have been enough non-student participants in the original group to provide for at least one in each of the two new

---

27. If he had not been a Sunday-school teacher, one of the authors would have been one of 125 members of a Sunday-school class while he was teaching at Goshen College. Members knew that the class was too large, but no one seemed to be able or willing to arrange for division.

groups. Our universal experience has been that members of groups of from fifteen to twenty-five members are not particularly eager to divide. (They are not divided if the committee cannot reach consensus or if there is a strong opposition within the group.) But the members of the two new groups are quite enthusiastic about the division afterward, and sometimes wonder why they did not divide earlier.

The way in which new small groups could be started at the opening of school in the fall was a subject of considerable discussion in the first year or two of these groups on the Bethel campus. The problem is not as great as it seems to be from a distance. At the end of each school year, evaluation retreats of steering committee members have been held. Tentative plans for core groups and subjects for consideration in the coming year have come to the surface in the retreat discussions. In the fall, the groups for the new school year have formed in the course of another retreat of former small-group members and interested students and during the first several weeks of the new school year. To the present, groups have formed primarily about core groups of people living near each other in the dormitory or acquainted with each other for other reasons, rather than about subjects proposed for discussion or action, although this does not have to be a precedent for the future. All, or almost all, groups have had both men and women in their memberships. In the second year of the small groups, when a large number of new groups had to be formed, three students simply asked every person present whom he would like to be with in the small groups for that year while everyone was eating the noon meal at a retreat held in the first week of school. Some people wanted to continue meeting with other members of small discussion groups that had just been held following a presentation, while others had made previous plans in their dormitories. In any case, the whole procedure of forming about eight or ten different core groups took only a little over an hour.

Small church groups on the Bethel campus have grown and divided often enough in the past several years to make continuity from year to year something of a problem. For the coming school year, members of existing small groups are planning to contact all new students personally in the dormitories during the first week of school. Former students will be asked to decide on the group in which they plan to participate during the first week of school; freshmen and new students may move around from group to group for three weeks before settling down and committing themselves to regular participation in a given small group.

Although the practice in the Bethel small groups has not been uniform to this point, both experience and considerations raised elsewhere in this paper seem to indicate the importance of asking small group members to express their commitment to Christ as well as their commitment to regular attendance. We have said enough in other contexts about the importance of a person's decision with respect to Christ. Asking for decision will divide the group participants into members, on one hand, and observers, on the other. Members and observers all commit themselves to regular attendance, but the former, the small-group-church members, witness also to their commitment to Christ. The church appropriately asks for a commitment of this kind on all of the levels of its functioning.

A prospective small-group-church participant, especially if he is a new student, may ask what the commitment to Christ implies. In a situation in which denominations overlap and cultural practices of Christians vary widely, this is not an unreasonable question. In fact, it is a part of the task of the church to determine what commitment to Christ implies in all of the new situations it confronts and on all of the levels of its functioning. In order not to prolong time spent in organization this last fall, however, the small group with which one of us was associated decided to use the baptismal vows in the General Conference Minister's Manual, with appropriate modifications, as the statement of its understanding of what being a member of the church and being committed to Christ implies. This procedure seemed appropriate and adequate for a beginning.

Small Churches Must Work Together in the Larger Church

The small church groups on the Bethel College campus have been known collectively as the Student Christian Fellowship. The Student Christian Fellowship, a congregation-sized unit, elects an executive committee (1) to function as a coordinating committee in aiding the individual groups, and (2) to sponsor general meetings of the whole Student Christian Fellowship membership.

A council, composed of one representative from the steering committee of each small church group and the members of the Student

Christian Fellowship Executive Committee, has met at approximately monthly intervals throughout the school year. The Executive Committee is an administrative body, as its name implies; the council serves as a forum at which ideas and problems are expressed and as an agency through which each group may be informed of the activities of the other groups.

The Student Christian Fellowship is a congregation-sized body made up of all of the student and non-student participants in the small church groups. Because it includes non-students, it might more appropriately be restructured to include other members of the college community and called the "College (or Campus) Christian Association," "Campus Christian Fellowship," or "Campus" Church. In any case, the Student Christian Fellowship is only one of several forms of the church of congregational size on or near the Bethel campus. (This situation is also characteristic of other Mennonite colleges.) We have already discussed the problem raised by the proliferation of church units or quasi-church units competing for students' interests on the college campus. It is partly for this reason that the total membership of the Student Christian Fellowship has met only rarely in general meetings on the Bethel campus in the past two or three years. The Student Christian Fellowship has sponsored voluntary chapel services which have been reasonably well attended. Suggestions for alleviating the problem produced by the multiplicity of units of congregational size on the campus were made in the earlier section of this paper in a discussion on the congregational life of students on campus.

The Student's Home Congregation

We are not among those who believe that church renewal can begin only with a more careful examination of or the setting of higher age requirements for baptismal candidates. The congregation must adequately demonstrate in its life the possibilities and obligations involved in the new life in Christ before baptismal candidates can properly decide whether they are ready to participate fully in that life or not—from one standpoint, congregational renewal is a prerequisite for setting higher expectations for baptismal candidates. The change of some baptismal practices may further the cause of congregational renewal, but it is only one of the many kinds of changes that can further this cause. In this paper, we are focusing our attention on what can be done for and with Mennonite college students, most of whom were baptized several years before college entrance. Our comments on home congregations and on baptismal practices will therefore be brief.

When a congregation has done all that it can to administer baptism properly, not as a device for getting the names of young people on the church roll and keeping them there, but as an honest confirmation of something that has actually occurred before God and man, it can then concern itself with the nature of the participation of the new church members in the congregations after baptism. Some congregations seem to lose touch with many of their young members in the years immediately following baptism. The pastor, who may have conducted the catechism class, turns his attention to other matters and other catechism classes, and the young Christians—with the non-Christians of their age—return to Sunday-school experiences of the kinds they knew before baptism. We would ask a question: Would there be ways in which the young Christians could meet from time to time to explore further the implications of their initial commitments? They do not need religious instruction alone; they need to grow more fully into the whole life of the church.

When they leave home for college, students should be asked to take statements concerning their standing in their home congregations and to ask for associate membership or membership in congregations near their places of study. In a society as mobile as the American society, students are not unique in moving from congregation to congregation. The expectation that a Christian will request membership or associate membership in a congregation near his place of residence can very appropriately be established when a student first leaves home for college.

We should make it easier for a student to indicate at one time or in one service his entrance as an associate member into congregation and small-group church at college. This could appropriately be done in a service in the congregation at the college in the fall. Home congregations and the college congregation should expect all Christian students to take this step. Situations arising when a student would want to retain his membership in his home congregation, a congregation he could not attend, and not express any interest in the church life on campus would, as we have previously noted, require careful handling and the cooperation of the pastor of the home congregation and representatives of the church on campus in an attempt to reach a clear understanding. All Christian students should be expected to participate in the life of the church while they are in college.

Students will normally attend their home congregations during college vacations when they are in their home communities. They may reasonably be expected to make contributions in Sunday school teaching, in youth fellowship leadership, and in other ways to their home congregations at such times. Some congregations ask each returned college student to say something in a public meeting about his concerns and interests as they have developed in college. Members of the community who have taken a few years of time from the world of work in order to pursue studies and to grow spiritually in special ways can very reasonably be expected to share some of the benefits of their study and growth with friends who have not been able to leave the home community for these purposes.

The Witness of the Church on Campus

The small churches and the student-faculty congregation are local manifestations of the church universal witnessing at a particular place and at a particular time to the lordship of Christ. Witnessing to Christ in word and deed is the primary function of the church in any situation. The first obligation of Christian students is to witness to Christ on the college campus. There will be a temptation to look for opportunities for Christian word and action off the campus. Without ruling out the place of the latter—and sometimes it may be very important—the campus remains the Christian student's first responsibility. He is best equipped to make a witness there, since he lives and shares in the life of the academic community. To present the Christian faith to his non-Christian roommates and friends as a dynamic, intellectually respectable, and comprehensive interpretation of reality is the commission the Christian college student has from his Lord.

The future leaders in the life of the nation will come from the colleges and universities. In many institutions of higher learning students rarely hear the call of the gospel which calls men into restored relationships with God and each other. This makes it all the more imperative that the claims of the gospel be presented clearly and without confusion in the Christian college. If this is not done the college may with some justification be called religious, but it has no right to masquerade under the name Christian, nor will the college be able convincingly to justify its continued existence on other than academic grounds.

Ecumenical Witness

The views expressed above, which are consonant with the Mennonite heritage and, we believe, also with the Scriptures, need to be voiced in the company of Christians of other traditions. We believe it introduces some order into a confused situation in Christian colleges, and that this is not at the expense of either Christian or academic integrity and freedom.

In the present crisis facing Christian liberal arts colleges, it is imperative that we attempt to put this proposal into practice. It may be that we should seriously consider in this connection the words of an executive of a large philanthropic corporation: "If the church colleges would dare to be loyal to the basic purpose of their existence they would lack neither students nor finance."[28] What this means basically is that people tend to take a clear-cut and demanding situation more seriously than one in which clarity of purpose and operation is lacking. Primarily, however, we ought to have the courage to implement this proposal because, as it appears to us, it flows directly out of the great commission and the mandate of Christ to His church.

This proposal has ecumenical implications for the broader perspective as well. Every year students graduate and take their places in society. The Christian students will also take their places in the church where they live and exert their influence. A number of the major denominations still deliberately perpetuate a modified form of the *Volkskirche* in which the distinction between church and world tends to be very uncertain. Graduates of a Mennonite Christian college should bear witness to the biblical and specifically New Testament delineation of the "people of God" as a community whose common loyalty is to the Lord Jesus Christ by personal confession in word and deed, and of a community in which by mutual discipline the tension between church and world is maintained.

28. Conway Boatman, "Task of Church-Related Colleges," *Christianity Today* 7 (May 10, 1963).

As James H. Nichols indicated in his Menno Simons lectures at Bethel College in January, 1963, there is at the present time an almost complete breakdown of church discipline. Although it is partly the cause, it is also partly the consequence of a blurring of the lines between church and world. The practice of discipline makes a working lay fellowship possible and prevents the church from becoming a clerical organization. By fostering such a disciplined fellowship in the college we help to train people who will more and more take their places in urban and suburban centers where contact with other Christians is a daily occurrence. They will be more able witnesses to the God who wants men to respond to Him freely and without constraint.

Only as we put into practice in the college the insights of our particular heritage is there any legitimization for perpetuating a Mennonite Christian college. We must not default at this point. To do so would be to betray our heritage.

Appendix 1
The Relevance of a Mennonite College's Right to Set Religious Standards

One argument sometimes used to oppose granting students the degree of freedom of choice suggested by this paper is phrased as follows: "We have a right to set religious standards for students who choose to attend our college. They do not have to come."

This argument can appropriately be used on counseling students who break standards they agreed on entrance to maintain—one can then focus attention on the broken agreement, rather than on the appropriateness of the standards themselves. All kinds of societies have written and unwritten standards, and a college is no exception.

This argument is beside the point, however, in decision as to whether given standards are appropriate for the ends the institution is trying to reach. Of course a college can demand what it wants. It could demand that all entering students should wear their overcoats on hot fall days or attend daily morning and evening prayer meetings or pay $2,000 per year tuition. The real question is: Does what the college demands really help it to achieve its ultimate goals? In the realm of religious objectives, does it help non-Christian students to understand the nature of God's call in Christ, and does it help Christian students grow spiritually? The thesis of the present paper is that having the same standards and expectations for Christian and for non-Christian students does not further these ends in the best way.

Appendix 2

The Relevance of the Fact That Most College Students Are Late Adolescents, Not Adults

The present paper assumes that most college students are in late adolescence and then proceeds to discuss the forms of church life appropriate to college young people in this state of their development.[29] Several comments on the relevance of the fact that most college students are late adolescents can be made here:

(1) Being in the church is never a matter of doing just what one pleases. The freedom discussed in the section "Freedom of Decision" is a freedom (1) to choose to join the church of Christ in the forms in which it presents itself in the local situation, or (2) not to choose to join the church of Christ in the situation in which one finds himself. Freedom in the church is not following one's day-to-day whims—it is accepting Jesus Christ as Lord and Master, and accepting the discipline of membership in His people. Adolescents do not just do what they please—in choosing between options A and B, they are choosing between two disciplines.

(2) There is an additional freedom in Christ and in the church: the freedom to make ethical decisions as the Holy Spirit leads. In this sense, the church determines what the content of its discipline shall be. The paper does not assume that the students will set the discipline in

---

29. See also Leonard Gross, "The Impact of Christian Education at the Various Age Levels: An Analysis of Pertinent Materials Written by the Leaders of Mennonite and Other Denominations, and a Review of Major Parochial School Systems of Other Denominations" (unpublished manuscript prepared for the Study Commission on Mennonite Secondary and Higher Education, Mennonite Board of Education, August, 1963). Gross considers primarily the structuring of Mennonite academic programs rather than the church life of students, the main focus of the discussion in the present paper.

Option B by themselves, however. The role of non-student members is referred to repeatedly.

A college congregation would include faculty members and possibly some other people in the immediate community, and these older leaders would be responsible for contributing from their learning and experience, just as they do in the academic community. If some students would not choose Option B, while most faculty members would, the faculty-to-student ratio in the spiritual community would be even higher than the academic community. The paper implies that, even though students were in the majority, structures could be developed in which the non-student participants in the campus congregation and in the individual small groups would adequately represent the voice of experience in these groups. This is now the case in the academic community. For example, students at Bethel College participate in making decisions concerning the structuring of academic life and the setting of graduation requirements through their Student Council representatives on the Educational Policies Committee—but they do not make these decisions alone. The faculty does not abdicate its responsibility just because the students make their fine contributions. Relationships with the church on the district and denominational levels would provide still other influence in the direction of stability and continuity, just as these relationships influence typical congregations in this way.

(3) Putting the main point briefly, however: either adolescents should not he baptized or they should be permitted and expected to identify themselves as Christians and to grow in the church, even though this will necessarily mean that they will be different in some ways from their non-Christian friends, Our experience has been that the great majority of students are mature enough to make serious religious decisions.

Appendix 3

The Mennonite Understanding of the Church and the Structure and Functioning of the Academic Community

In this paper we have assumed the existence of present Mennonite academic structures and then asked how the church can best function in the context of these structures. We have not raised the very important question as to the relevance of Mennonite understandings for the structuring of Mennonite academic programs.

One of the present authors has indicated elsewhere some of the considerations that need further study.[30] Here we will only indicate more or less at random, some specific questions that might be raised. To take an obvious example, the importance Mennonites attach to the place of the church in history should influence the range of curricular offerings and the vocational counseling in the college they sponsor. To take a more perplexing example, some of the considerations dictating an appropriate upper limit to the size of a congregation may also set an upper limit to the size of a small-college unit that can function in the best way as an academic community. It is not that this would dictate a limit to the size of each of the units within a larger institution. There could be a college structure of the type found in English universities or at Wesleyan University in Connecticut even though the total institution was much larger. If the Mennonite college at a given location were regarded as a single unit, however, it would seem that the upper limit for a congregation-like community might be somewhat lower than the level at which the institution might be most effectively operated. As a very rough guess, it has been suggested that a typical liberal arts college offering the usual variety of majors should have from eight hundred to one thousands students[31] for efficient operation. If this is true, Mennonites would have to choose whether (1) to operate economically, or (2) to operate somewhat inefficiently in order to have the advantages of a small academic community.

The founding of Conrad Grebel College in Waterloo, Ontario, also raises a question: What cooperative relationships between Mennonite college units and other colleges and universities best express our Mennonite understanding of the task of the church in higher education? At their best, Anabaptists and Mennonites have held that the truths by which congregations should live were not only certain beliefs transmitted from generation to generation or discovered as entities that would have had a previously disincarnate existence; they are also arrived at and formulated in specific situations through a process of intensive

---

30. Albert J. Meyer, "Needed: A Mennonite Philosophy of Higher Education," *Mennonite Life* 17 (1962) 3.

31. This figure is really very uncertain—it depends on many unspecified variables.

research and conversation under the leadership of the Holy Spirit. The understanding of truth will certainly influence the search for truth on a Mennonite college campus. The communication of values to a student in the classroom, in counseling, and in extracurricular activities might well involve his own active participation in the process of their discovery and formulation. What we have said about truth would also imply that interpersonal relationships within the academic community are very important.

Some scholars have seen in the Anabaptist practice of searching for consensus under the leading of the Holy Spirit historical roots of the much less personal process of arriving at consensus on political questions in modern democratic states. The relationship between life in the church and life in the state is probably primarily one of analogy; the relationship between the spiritual community and the academic community is probably also one of analogy. In each case, there are fundamental differences between the communities. At the same time, it is one of the functions of the church in larger societies of every kind to demonstrate the possibilities in human social life in God's world.

We recognize the tentative character and inadequacy of these comments. We would conclude with the words of the previously cited article:

> Let us still hope for the day when the Holy Spirit will break forth in power and the very structures and fundamental objectives of our institutions will be shaped into forms that reflect more adequately our best Christian insights.[32]

---

32. Meyer, "Needed," 4

5

The Bethel Experience in Retrospect

Joanne Zerger Janzen

My three years in the small Christian fellowship groups at Bethel College continue to be valuable to me in several ways. While participating in these groups which we called seminars, I began to discover a religion more valid for me than the one I had been practicing. This is a kind of Christianity which calls me to live in a loving, forgiving relationship with as many persons as possible and to help them become their best, potential selves. This involves persons related to me in widely diverse ways—the children in Jordan who need milk and my home church member, my unpleasant neighbor lady and my graduate student friends, my parents and the Congolese student who needs a French teacher. The means to fulfill this call also are ones of personal contact. The Christian community seeks, in Christ's spirit, to help its member define what his call means in particular situations; the community's encouragement and forgiveness give him enough confidence and security to risk following this call. This is a contrast to my earlier belief that being Christian was essentially a private project undertaken by oneself with God's help and that one could establish the right personal relationship with God independent of other people. The call to commit myself to the task of reconciling separated people has helped unify my religious beliefs and the purpose in my life.

The discovery of the social nature of Christianity came to me largely through a group of Christians, our seminar, who shared their insights, questions, and past experiences concerning the Christian life. I learned at least as much from what our group tried to be as from what we discussed. We tried to act and make our decisions according to the truth that emerged from our conversation and the conviction that came out of our worship. One year our fellowship tried to follow through on our discussion of communion by deciding whether we should take this sacrament in some form in our own informal church. Members made an effort to talk out and forgive the grudges between themselves and others. We tried to assist each other with practical problems. Several fellow seminar members and I confronted with the choice of a major were guided by the consequent seminar sessions on Christian decision-making and vocation. With the aid of the principles and approaches outlined in the weekly meeting, several friends and I could talk through the very specific pros and cons of my choosing an English major. The most personal and the most important guidance and support that seminar members gave each other often took place in such discussions between two or three members.

My enthusiasm for our serious Christian fellowship grew because here Christianity seemed to be alive. Right action and belief for particular situations were determined by the group seeking God's will, rather than from rules for the Christian life. This idea of Christian discipleship has made me more free to do God's will and to thereby find myself because the right thing to do must continually be determined anew; I do not become so restricted by an inflexible commitment, for example, to being a chemistry major or an English teacher, when I could better do God's will in a different way. I also credit the fellowship for making me more persistent in my own Christian searching and discipline. The seminar discussions gave my efforts added significance; the concern of fellow members who felt some responsibility for me encouraged and aided me; and the help and interest they expected from me made me less negligent in giving the help they needed.

My seminar experience was valuable because here I found out experientially what my heritage from the Anabaptists was. Our seminar studied the Anabaptist concept of the church and Christian discipleship, and then tried to embody in our own group what we found helpful from their ideas and experiences. In this way I developed an appreciation and enthusiasm for my religious ancestry that I would not have gained through a detached investigation of them.

I value my experience with the Bethel seminars for what they tried to be, even though we frequently failed to drive discussions through to decisions or to be as open and honest as we could have been or to deal directly with barriers that developed within our group. But from our occasional successes I realize what quality of Christian living close fellowship groups could make possible, and so I am grateful to the Bethel seminars for an ideal, which I tried to sketch in the preceding paragraphs.

Our shortcomings also have taught me some things to watch for in my future participation in Christian fellowships. Speculative philosophic and theological discussions often left behind those members lacking a philosophic bent or the right background of reading and sometimes kept those carrying the discussions from directly confronting more personal and important issues. Sessions on practical problems, such as anger toward those dorm-mates whose noise disturbed us, were the discussions in which we had the most common experiences and interests and the least difficulty making ourselves understood.

Our seminar experience underlined the necessity of giving our fellowship continual attention. For members to develop a Christian responsibility for each other, we needed to spend more time than the weekly seminar hour learning to know and trust each other. We needed a steering committee which met before each seminar session to plan the next meeting. It was important that the steering committee define a current version of members' interests, consider the internal problems and the purpose and direction of the seminar, and investigate issues external to the group with which it should be concerned. All of these can shift quickly for a group of college students; the question a student places on the discussion agenda at the first of the year may no longer be his life concern when the seminar is scheduled to take it up. In order to keep the fellowship effective, the committee must keep in constant touch with all members to inform them of the plans for the next meeting, to show concern for their absences, and to get the feedback of ideas about what the seminar is and ought to be doing.

One problem to our seminars was the fringe member, who did not commit himself to regular, active participation, although the group asks this of its members. It hurt those of us who were enthusiastic about our small fellowship to know that others could indifferently take or leave something so important to us. It took extra effort and often frustrating conversations to continually bring the fringe member up-to-date on the seminar developments since he last attended, especially if he eventually dropped out anyway. As a result I think these irregular attendees were sometimes wrongly blamed for the hesitancy of the regular members to share the more important sides of themselves or for general lack of enthusiasm and effort in the seminar. The seminar is responsible for accommodating in some way persons not yet ready to commit themselves to the fellowship, and I have observed in our close Christian fellowship at the University of Kansas that when regular members feel themselves a part of a vital, significant fellowship and are able to be open with each other, then visitors do not interfere or detract from the meeting, but rather are caught up by its spirit. The value of my Bethel seminar experience has made me eager to be part of a similar group in the new communities where I will live.

6

Christian Life at Conrad Grebel College

WALTER KLAASSEN

The Congregational Program

Introduction

This account will be a personal account for two reasons. First, because the work of the chaplaincy was put into my hands alone, and, secondly, because I understood that I was to give shape to the chaplaincy at Conrad Grebel College; no program, no specific plan of action was proposed by anyone.

I had many conversations with Dr. J. W. Fretz, Dr. Albert Meyer, and others about the work I was undertaking prior to my coming to Waterloo. My experience at Bethel College with small study and fellowship groups had given me some basic clues as to what might be done. The production of *Church and Mennonite College* together with Albert Meyer during 1963–64 had greatly helped me in clarifying certain matters relating to my prospective work, especially in my view of the church and its purpose, and how the church might best be practically realized in a college situation. The basic principles of the Anabaptist heritage were spelled out in that document. We were convinced that the Anabaptist vision of the church was viable in the twentieth century, and determined that, so far as it was our responsibility, we would work toward a modern realization of that vision. It should perhaps be said here that, although I have a theological education, I am a layman, never having been ordained.

What follows now is an account of what has developed in the area of Christian activity in the college since September, 1964. At the end I will raise some questions about the direction of the program as it now exists and to point out some areas in which nothing, or virtually nothing, has been done.

Suppositions and Basic Intentions

Basic to my work as I envisaged it before I came was the view of the church that I had adopted which I believed to be the intention of the New Testament and of the Anabaptist-Mennonite tradition. I was encouraged in my intention to attempt a realization of this view of the church by the fact that most of the actual experiments in church renewal now in progress in America, and much recent writing about the church in the world, coincide with our tradition. (Readers are referred especially to Collin Williams's *Where in the World and What in the World*, which provide both theological analyses as well as actual examples.) I was concerned not merely to be an individual "religious" counselor and to be on the council of SCM and IVCF; I was concerned not merely about providing groping students with intellectual rationale for Christian faith. I was concerned that while these were my responsibility they be placed into the context of an actual growing Christian community. I was concerned to do what lay in my power to actualize the church, the community of Christian faith, in a relevant way among the members of the University of Waterloo that chose to live at Conrad Grebel College. I was concerned, therefore, not to disperse my energies by spreading them thinly over 3,000 students, but to concentrate on the hundred who lived together under this roof.

I believe that the church is the company of the disciples of Christ, bound together in common loyalty to Christ, and which under the guidance of His Spirit is a servant to the world even as Jesus Christ was a servant. To be a servant to the world means to know and to understand its needs. It means also the marshaling of all the resources within the servant church to meet the needs that actually exist, and then to proceed to deal with them insofar as it is able. Sessions of study, prayer, and fellowship where the spirit of Christ can lead committed people into new understanding of the world and its needs as well as of themselves as individuals who have gifts that can be employed in Christ's service to the world are indispensable. This means that I do not regard the parish pattern of church life as normative for every situation but that new forms need to be devised to meet new situations.

I had no clear idea when I came what the form suited to this situation might be, and was prepared to let the situation itself dictate the pattern and write the agenda for us. I did hope to initiate some small fellowship and study groups. I came with one (to me) very important assumption. This was that both the biblical as well as the Anabaptist-Mennonite tradition insist that persons must be accorded the maximum freedom possible in deciding whether to be disciples of Jesus Christ or not. Members of CGC would thus be asked to declare themselves as Christians or non-Christians. No person who could not declare himself a Christian would be required to participate in the activity of the Christian community. Even Mennonite students should here have the freedom to opt out of Christian activity if they felt compelled to do so.

What Actually Happened in 1964–65

Before our first academic year was very far along certain factors relating to the forming of a Christian community at CGC began to emerge. The first was of a practical nature. It was difficult for CGC members to get to city churches on Sunday morning because of a complete lack of transportation. The nearest church was a mile away, the nearest Mennonite church a bit farther. The second factor was the suggestion of a number of students that since we had a fine chapel at the College, we ought to have regular Sunday worship services for the CGC community. A survey of student opinion revealed considerable interest in the proposal. About the middle of September, 1964, a meeting of local Mennonite ministers was called to discuss the matter and to counsel the chaplain and student representatives. It was the consensus of the group that a service of worship should be instituted on Sunday morning at 9:30. The early hour would still enable students to attend churches in the Twin Cities. This arrangement was to be carried forward on a trial basis until approximately Christmas at which time it was to be subject to reevaluation.

When a late December meeting brought out only two representatives of the Mennonite ministry, we agreed unilaterally to continue college worship services but to change the time from morning to evening. This was done for three reasons. First, it would enable students who had responsibilities in their home congregations in the morning to become part of the student congregation with a good conscience. Second, it would enable students to visit Twin City worship services in the morning. Finally, it would enable me to become involved with my family in a Twin City congregation on Sunday morning.

Every student at CGC had been invited at the beginning of the year to have a conversation with me about his religious views and affiliations. About 75 percent of the students responded.

As soon as the worship program began we also began to meet for an hour of discussion and study in the hour following. The sermon quickly became the subject of study. A committee had been elected during the first term to meet with me during the week to plan the following Sunday's program. This quickly included the decision about a sermon topic. This procedure enabled us to concentrate on issues that occupied students' minds. It was a great help to me and deeply involved those students who met with me and also the congregation to the degree that its concerns were taken up by the committee. Student involvement in planning also made for more intensive participation in discussion later. Attendance at worship services averaged about thirty to thirty-five throughout the year and about twelve to fifteen for the study sessions. Attendance was about evenly divided between Mennonite and non-Mennonite students. Offerings were received at the worship services during the second term most of which was given to MCC for a specified purpose.

Because of the newness and the novelty of a student congregation many students, including Mennonites, found it difficult to take the whole matter seriously. The study group tended to change in personnel from Sunday to Sunday, making continuous study on any one subject very difficult. On the whole, Mennonite teenagers are expected to be seen in church but not heard, an expectation which too many of those who attended conformed to. Then there were also those who were neither heard nor seen. We were often frustrated by the feeling of playing at church. Consequently, it cannot be said that we managed actually to form a Christian congregation. There existed no real conviction of oneness. On a few occasions toward the end of the year we seemed to be moving toward our goal, but before we could take more concrete steps, the year was over. Student comments about the experiment, however, were encouraging. Some saw what was being attempted, and this first year's experience was basic to subsequent developments.

Preparing for 1965–66

Organized Student Congregation Proposed

Discussions with Dr. Fretz and students and considerable reflection on basic intentions and suppositions with which I came and the experiences of the first year led to a specific proposal for the formation of a student Christian congregation. The details of the proposal were contained in a letter to all students accepted for residence.

1. A covenant service on one of the first Sundays in which all those who are Christians would pledge to each other that for these seven months they will be the church in CGC and on the campus of the University of Waterloo, and a commitment to regular attendance at worship and study session of the church.

2. A formal membership roll for the seven months, but with the possibility of receiving new members during the year.

3. Membership in the CGC church would be renewed at the beginning of every year. This means that there would be no continued congregation during the summer months.

4. Full membership for the seven months, not associate membership. This would mean that most students would be full members in their home churches as well as in the CGC church. There will be no transfer of membership from the home church to the CGC church.

5. Election of deacons and other personnel to give guidance to the program of the church.

6. The celebration of the Lord's Supper and the practice of church discipline. The meaning of church discipline here is the conscious and deliberate assumption of responsibility by the members of the church for each other for mutual help and encouragement in Christian commitment.

7. The regular receiving of an offering and the performance of some needed service in the community.
8. A mutual search for God's will under the guidance of the spirit of Christ. The community together grapples with ethical and social problems while seeking guidance in the Scriptures.

Letters similar to those sent to students were sent to all ministers of all Ontario Mennonite churches and to the ministers of non-Mennonite students accepted for residence, explaining our program and enlisting their support in encouraging their young people to join the CGC church. Because of the presence of non-Mennonite students such a church would not set up any specific Mennonite standards for membership, especially since it would be a temporary church. Mennonite ministers were asked to submit names of members attending schools in the area other than Conrad Grebel that they too might be served by the college church.

Three responses were received from ministers, two Mennonite, one United Church of Canada. Two were positive and encouraging. One of the Mennonite respondents (not from Ontario) was extremely irritated by the whole thing, accusing me of assuming that nothing was being done for the spiritual welfare of Mennonite young people in their home churches. Apart from these responses there has been "neither praise nor blame" from the constituency served by the college.

Chaplain's Assistant

At the end of the 1964–65 academic year I proposed the appointment of a chaplain's assistant with a view to greater participation of the proposed congregation especially in worship on Wednesdays and Sundays. The proposal came partly because of the potential availability of a senior student who had proved himself extraordinarily capable of relating to CGC students as a Christian. He would help me keep in touch with the current questions and subjects of discussion in the house and alert me to situations where counseling and help was needed. He would also be directly involved in preparing for and leading in worship and study on Wednesdays and Sundays. It was proposed that he be given a $200 bursary as remuneration for his time. This proposal was endorsed by the President and the Chairman of the Board and the consent of John Rempel, Kitchener, to render this service was gained.

Events of 1965–66 to the Present

Evidently the proposal for the formation of a student congregation caught the imagination of a considerable number of students. About seventy came out to the first announced worship service on September 19. After the worship period I further explained the idea of a student congregation, and answered a number of questions. No decision was taken, but there appeared to be plenty of enthusiasm.

Discussing the Nature of the Church

On the advice of a voluntary committee of students it was decided that I preach a sermon or two on the nature of the church and to relate this directly to our situation. This aided in further clarifying for interested students just what was involved. Emphasis was laid on voluntary commitment not only to the idea and actual membership but to regular participation in the meetings and activities of the congregation. Concern was expressed by some about occasional responsibilities elsewhere and occasional visits home. Such absences, it was agreed, were not our concern, and were quite compatible with membership. What we were concerned to emphasize was that membership in this congregation should not be regarded as a casual, unimportant matter with attendance at congregational meetings subject to the whim of the moment.

The main reason for establishing a congregation with actual membership was that it would give some objective form to our mutual responsibility for each other. It was not to be an attempt to create uniformity but unity; it was to help the realization of a visible Christian community in which individuals could speak to each other in honesty without fear of being labeled, and thus to grow in faith, the understanding of Christian commitment, and the implications of it.

Confession of Faith

It became clear that coming together as a Christian community we would need some clarity on the central matters of Christian faith. I was commissioned to prepare a sermon on the topic, which was then thoroughly discussed in small-group sessions. It was decided in committee to advance the three main points as a confession of faith of the congregation. The statement was worked on by a special committee and then presented to the whole group where more discussion took place. It was accepted with some significant modifications as the confessional basis of the proposed congregation. The statement is as follows:

> We confess that human beings everywhere act on selfish motives which ultimately injure and destroy others, and that this constitutes a denial of God; that only Jesus Christ, by virtue of His own complete obedience to God's will can deliver men from sin and set them free for constructive and responsible living;
>
> that man's deliverance from sin provides for him the possibility to live freely and responsibly in a community of persons, the church that here he learns the meaning of forgiveness, and may, together with others, discover the will of God;
>
> that the church is commissioned to call all men to obedience to the living Christ and to live and act in the world in love and reconciliation, following the example of Jesus, even to the point of giving its life for others, and that such service is not lost because Jesus Christ is the Lord of history.

Formation of a Congregation

On October 17, we had a service of commitment that was in the form of a covenant of the members with each other and with God. The act of commitment consisted of signing our names in a book laid on the communion table. Fifty-five students signed their names on that occasion to form the congregation. Six others have joined since then; one student has voluntarily withdrawn because regular attendance is prevented by responsibilities in his home church. Present membership is sixty.

Membership in the CGC congregation is therefore full membership with all of its responsibilities, although most members also retain membership in their home congregations. It is quite evident that this Christian congregation is taken seriously both by its members and by nonmembers in the college. There has, up to this point, been no indication of cliquishness. Conversations about Christian faith in the house regularly involve nonmembers, and the Sunday meetings are normally about 30 percent nonmembers. The congregational membership is 62 percent Mennonite, the rest being Anglican, Lutheran, United Church of Canada, Presbyterian, Baptist, E.U.B., Pentecostal, Society of Friends, United Missionary Church. It includes five nonresident students. The Mennonite group is made up of Mennonite Church, Western Ontario Mennoite, General Conference, and Mennonite Brethren.

Organization and Program

The Sunday after the formation of the congregation a few organizational steps were taken. A treasurer, several secretaries, and a coffee committee were elected. A rotating advisory committee for the weekly planning of congregational meetings and for the formulation of proposals was provided for, John Rempel being in charge of the weekly convening of this committee. The reason for this arrangement is that it is inequitable to expect one group of people to meet every week to do all the planning work. It also has the distinct advantage of involving all the members of the congregation at one time or another in the actual planning of the congregation's activities. Special committees are appointed as needed. One such committee is working at present on questions regarding the form and content of our worship services, and specifically, the use of hymns and prayers.

The weekly program begins with a committee meeting on Tuesday evening at 10:00 PM. Regular members are John Rempel, Walter Klaassen, Everett Mossman (residence director and senior seminarian at Waterloo Lutheran Seminary). The main question is the theme for the following Sunday's activities. Various ideas or concerns may be presented, arising out of some personal concern, out of some event in the university or the world, or some question that is alive in the house. It may be in doctrine, ethics, politics, or social problems. A topic is decided upon by consensus and some discussion follows to narrow it down so that it becomes quite specific.

On Sunday evening at seven we begin with a formal worship service in semi-traditional style, varying the order to suit the subject and the worship materials employed. After the hymn following the sermon there may be a short congregational meeting to deal with some proposal. Decisions at such meetings are always reached by consensus. Votes have been taken only in the election of personnel. After the congregational meeting we go into the dining hall for coffee and biscuits, spending an hour or so in discussion of the evening's sermon. If a decision is called for the leaders of the groups (usually about five or six) report at the end, and again decision is by consensus. If consensus is not possible, the matter may be discussed further or postponed for a week. The whole meeting ends with prayer and benediction.

The Wednesday meetings at 7:00 PM are also an integral part of the congregational program with the content varying widely. It may focus on a meditation, on some problem in the house or congregation; it may be a congregational meeting for decision, it may be a prayer meeting, or a session for confrontation with some world problem or way to meet it. My assistant and I alternate in preparing for and leading these meetings. We maintain considerable flexibility in our meetings in terms of time and in taking account of other events on campus and beyond. We may defer our Wednesday chapel service hour to a good film or a lecture and hold it at some other hour. On Sunday, January 30, the congregation went as a group to hear Dr. Willard Krabill speak on Vietnam. Sometimes meetings are simply canceled when conflicts cannot be resolved.

The Lord's Supper

This subject deserves special attention because of the way in which some serious difficulties connected with the celebration of the Eucharist by an ecumenical congregation without an ordained clergyman were resolved. This matter had been discussed at the very beginning of the year, but other matters had delayed a decision at that time. In any case it was felt that some sense of congregational unity would have to develop before we could seriously consider it. The matter was raised briefly just before Christmas, and was then made the subject for the first Sunday's meeting in January. I preached on the subject, emphasizing strongly the eucharistic-community aspects of the Supper and by implication deemphasizing the sacramental-memorial aspects. A vigorous discussion lasting well over an hour followed, ending in a unanimous decision to celebrate the Supper together at the earliest opportunity.

The suggestion that an ordained minister be invited to help us was rejected because it would be incongruous with our emphasis on the committed fellowship, and would introduce a sacramental element which we were anxious to avoid. A committee was appointed to draw up plans for the Lord's Supper and the preparation of a liturgy was put in the hands of the chaplain. It was decided that the bread and wine would be served by the members to each other with the appropriate words. The actual celebration on Sunday, January 23, was a high point of our congregational life. We all stood around the table and in the signs of bread and wine rejoiced that we had been made into a genuine human community by the Spirit of Christ.

Peace Witness

Much of the peace activity on the campus of this university originates in this congregation. I have had several opportunities to speak on the subject. Several of our members are deeply involved in the Student Union for Peace Action, which is the Canadian counterpart of SDA. We are well represented on a peace study group that has begun to meet on the campus, and which, according to rumor, the communists have already infiltrated. Several members of the congregation went to Washington for the big march. They were, in fact, the only representatives from this campus. We have made contact with several Friends who are on the faculty and who are busy in peace work. It is very exciting, particularly to see the students so busy at it. One of our members, a non-Mennonite, is by far the most active and intense in his dedication. He became a Christian here last year and seems to have become a pacifist at the same time.

Student Reaction

Student reaction to this program generally has been positive. Attendance at meetings has increased so that congregations of seventy to ninety people on Sunday evening are not uncommon. Both members and nonmembers in CGC take the program seriously. It leads to animated discussion in the house involving almost all of the students at one time or another. Nominal Christians have begun to ask questions about their relation to Christ. Some have concluded that, though they are baptized they are not Christians. Others are being challenged to give Christian faith serious consideration.

Evaluation and Questions

The year 1965-66 up to this point has been an unusually exciting and rewarding experience. I am amazed at the genuine interest and involvement of such a large number of our residents. It is, I believe, in large measure to be attributed to the provision of maximum freedom for decision, and also to the readiness of our members to respond when they are asked to make the decisions and are given the confidence that they are in fact fully capable of doing so.

There is no question in my mind that CGC students are being helped in their Christian commitment by this program. They are continually asking questions about the meaning of Christian affirmations and of their implications for personal and communal life. There is evidence of growing understanding of the central significance of Christ and of what the church is both among members and nonmembers, Christians and non-Christians. The ecumenical dimension has fostered a readiness to listen to those of other traditions. Here is the ecumenical movement at the grass roots.

A day-long retreat is planned by the congregation for the end of the year to evaluate the year's experience and to plan for next year. Concern has already been expressed to provide for some means of establishing continuity through the summer months, so that it will not be necessary to repeat all the steps taken last fall. The main questions to be raised with respect to the role of CGC in Christian service to students are in my estimation as follows:

1. Arc we on the right path to concentrate our efforts so exclusively on the CGC community? What about the Mennonite students in the University of Waterloo, Waterloo Lutheran University?
2. Is the congregational program in CGC preventing CGC students from actively participating in the campus Christian groups, IVCF and SCM? Should we defer study and action programs to these organizations?
3. Should CGC make itself responsible for chaplaincy service to the Mennonite students at other Ontario universities?
4. Is the CGC program having adverse effects on the relationship of the student to his home congregation, especially if it is nearby?
5. Is the CGC program helping to prepare the student to assume a responsible role in his home or any other congregation upon completion of his time here?

Counseling

Pastoral counseling by the chaplain now appears to be an adjunct to the congregational as well as to the Instructional Program. (See below.)

There is no great rush of students seeking out the chaplain for counseling. I believe that students must come on their own initiative, and this factor determines the number of counseling sessions. There have been many serious discussions, averaging, I would guess, at several a week. Quite a few CGC students have never been in my office for a serious talk about questions or problems.

Many students go to my assistant instead, and this is perhaps the greatest value of the assistantship. It also provides a way into my office, if necessary, that might otherwise not be there. The results of counseling are difficult to assess on the whole. All one can do is hope that some help has been given. Sometimes a student will identify an area in or a problem with which he has received help. Usually this is not the case.

The Instructional Program

Two religious knowledge courses carrying credit as Arts electives in the University of Waterloo are offered by Conrad Grebel College. Religious Knowledge 100G (Christian Foundations) is an introductory course in the Old Testament and the Synoptic Gospels. It seeks to provide a unified view of the development of our Christian heritage from the history and faith of Israel through the teachings and ministry of Jesus. Religious Knowledge 210G (Christian Heritage) is a study in the history of the Christian church. There was strong emphasis in the early formative period on the basis of the New Testament literature, on developments in form and doctrine during the first five centuries, and the Reformation, special attention being given to the Anabaptist movement by comparison to Roman Catholic, Anglican, Lutheran, and Reformed Christianity. Twenty-six registered in RK 100G and eighteen in RK 210G. (These are 1964–65 figures. The figures for 1965–66 are twenty-nine and twenty-four respectively.) Most of these were Conrad Grebel College students.

My approach to teaching the course in Bible is open-ended. Rather than approaching the Bible dogmatically as God's Word, and which on this view is in a class all by itself, being neither literature nor history in the common meaning of those terms, I try to allow the Bible to speak as the record of the religious experience of an actual nation in space and time, and to show that what is presented there represents an approach to the nature of reality that has a right to serious consideration by university students. I am only too well aware of the problems entailed by such an approach. Many students assume that there is only one way of approaching the Bible and experience profound frustration in my class. Sometimes this leads to a complete closing of the mind with the probable result that prejudices are encouraged and confirmed. Sometimes it leads to a despairing agnosticism. Usually it leads to a gratifying liberation in that it enables growth in religious understanding to keep pace with the general growth in apprehension at the university.

Although the classroom is not an evangelistic tent, this approach to the Bible forced some basic questions to the surface toward the end of the year. The main one was, "Who is Jesus Christ?" Three sessions were spent in question and answer, the class itself pushing the instructor to clarify in some detail the Christian understanding of Jesus Christ. This would have been done in any event, but I believe the method of approach almost necessarily pushed the class into asking the question. To speak to questions that demand an answer is pedagogically more productive than for the instructor to pose the question abstractly and then proceed to answer it. If the student asks the question it will usually not be suited to the answer the instructor has prepared for the way in which he would have asked the question. My hope is that those in the class who call themselves Christians will be more aware of the nature and demand of their commitment, and that those who are not Christians will also better understand what Christian faith is.

RK 210G does not have quite the combustible properties of 100G, but my approach is the same. While I am concerned that students know some of the facts of church history, I am also concerned that they know something of the reasons for those facts. They should know, for example, that while the Gospel of John is for many Christians the most important New Testament book, the author's use of current religious and philosophical vocabulary was partly responsible for leading the church directly into a theological compromise with Platonic metaphysics which bedevils the theological scene even today. They should know that the Christian church also exemplifies man's desire to separate religion from ethics, to move the center of gravity in man's relationship to God from the ethical and concrete to the sacramental and abstract. They should know that generally accepted Christian participation in war did not emerge until after the church and state entered into partnership under Constantine and his successors, and that the Christian doctrine of the just war became necessary only after Christians began to see the defense of the empire as synonymous with the defense of the church. They should know that the Anabaptists were the theological demythologizers of the sixteenth century, and that their descendants, provided they are true to the genius of their forebears, are in the best possible position to deal with twentieth-century fashions both in theology and ethics.

Those reflections were prepared last May, but hold for this year's activities as well. The validity of this approach may, of course, be questioned. Is this approach the one most likely to achieve the results envisaged by those who conceived the idea of the college? Perhaps we should abandon the teaching of courses like this and concentrate on helping students to evaluate from a Christian perspective their engineering, biology, history, and philosophy courses. This would, however, necessitate a change in, or addition to, present faculty.

The proposed department of religious studies to be set up in the university, with the college supplying the faculty, raises these and other questions relative to our present instructional program in religious knowledge. Since this is not yet a reality, however, and since no detailed proposals have been prepared to date, discussion would be premature.

7

The Bluffton College Christian Fellowship

Henry Rempel

Historical Background

The desire to form a Christian fellowship on the Bluffton College campus first arose during the second semester of the 1964–65 school year. There was considerable interest in the idea with thirty or more students participating in the initial discussions on the issue. It took some time and considerable effort to determine what should be the nature of the fellowship. After this had been decided it was even more difficult for each individual to decide whether he wanted to accept the responsibility of being a member. Eventually, with only a few weeks left in the semester, some fifteen students, several faculty members, and a pastor from a local Mennonite church entered into a relationship of commitment with each other. The nature of this relationship was based on the acceptance of the following statement:

> Outline of the Commitment to the New College Fellowship
>
> A. We commit ourselves to the lordship of Christ. This commitment is based on the conviction that man reaches that potential intended for him by his Creator-God only when man is

in a love relationship with that God. This love relationship is to be found in man's voluntary response in obedience to the love of Jesus of which he is becoming aware.

B. We commit ourselves to involvement with the group responding in obedience to the lordship of Christ.

Implicit in this commitment is:

1. The free giving and receiving of all that can be beneficially shared in our search for obedience.
2. Individual responsibility for the total well-being of the members of the group.
3. Individual obedience to the group's understanding of what would be the will of God in any given situation.

There were no scheduled meetings during the summer, but upon returning to the campus for the Fall semester, students immediately set about the task of forming a similar group to continue the experience of the previous year. All interested people were invited to participate. The initial discussions included most of the previous year members still on campus plus a number of other students who had heard glowing reports and were coming to investigate for themselves. The experience of the previous year could not be readily reproduced, and a major disagreement arose over the nature of the fellowship. As a result, interest lagged and attendance at discussions dropped considerably. The area of disagreement proved to be such a major obstacle that no move toward an established membership was made until December. The basis of this new relationship was the acceptance of the following statement:

> A Proposed Basis for Establishing a Bond
> of Christian Fellowship
>
> The Bible makes the claim that man becomes a new creation as he enters into relationship with the God made known in Christ Jesus. In our desire to know this experience of new creation we, as a fellowship, agree to search diligently for this God and to respond in obedience as He makes himself known. Recognizing that God works through people, we see it as imperative to be to each other vehicles through which God can make His will known so that we will be faithful in continuing Christ's work of reconciling man to God.

The Reason for Existence

The decision to form a Christian fellowship was based on the interaction of two concerns. The first was the search by individual students for at least relative security and some meaning in life in the midst of a series of endless assignments which served primarily to disrupt their lives. The second concern was one for fellow students on campus and other people in the surrounding community.

The search for security was the more immediate concern, and therefore, should be considered the initiating force in the formation of the group. Participants in a church-related college tend to come from a religious background, so it is not surprising that a search for security should be centered in a desire to relate to God. The fellowship was to be an environment which would better enable each member to respond in obedience to God as He made Himself known. Such a solution to the problem of insecurity implied several theological presuppositions. Some of the participants in the initial discussions found these too limiting and ceased to continue.

The mission concern arose out of a recognition that obedience to God would mean being active in God's redemptive activity. During the first year this concern helped to determine the nature of the group, and as such proved to be a healthy balance to the selfish search for security. The initial concern for personal security was turned into a desire to serve God, which meant service to our fellowmen.

During the second year these same two concerns existed, but each tended to be centered in different individuals. The result was a division of the group into two groups. It was not merely that some were selfishly seeking security while others had a mission concern, but rather, the issue was to determine the nature of the fellowship needed to implement these two concerns. Was the purpose for fellowship meetings to serve the members or was it for the purpose of engaging in mission? This division resulted in a series of meetings which proved most disruptive and prevented the effective formation of a committed fellowship.

These two viewpoints were not mutually exclusive, so the conflict would not have been serious had there been a method for decision-making and overcoming divergent viewpoints. Such a procedure did not exist, so in the face of rapidly declining attendance the solution was to concentrate on the content of the meetings so that attendance would be worthwhile. Those of interest to participants were discussed. These included such topics as death, how one knows the will of God, who God is, and why believe in God. This approach tended to alienate those who saw a binding commitment as essential for further action as a church. The compromise finally reached and was the preparation of a statement of commitment which then served as the basis for determining membership for the 1965–66 school year. All those prepared to accept this commitment joined together in a binding relationship through participation in a meeting set aside for this purpose.

Initially it had been a conscious decision to limit the existence of the fellowship to one school year at a time and to avoid written constitutions. This intention was to avoid an organization with a set program that merely invited participation. Existence was to be dependent solely on members wanting to be a church. To break every summer enabled reformation when this was necessary. In the light of our experience this year, this may prove to be an idealistic and inefficient approach. With some participants having previous experience and others being totally new to the idea, the desire to form a structure acceptable to all demanded considerable effort, comparable to that of the first year. This year too many things were taken for granted, so for several months, as a group, we had no reason for existence.

The Nature of the Fellowship

The most obvious expression of the Christian fellowship on the Bluffton campus has been the weekly meetings. These have been unstructured, with little prior planning and no appointed or elected leadership. The major exception has been several worship services planned in the form of a communion service. The purpose for existence was a joining together to know what it means to be obedient to God, so the necessity for meeting was self-evident. Structured leadership was avoided with the hope of preventing attendance with expectation of being served. Each participant was to attend with the realization that the proceedings of the meeting were partly dependent on his contribution.

The purpose of the communion services was primarily to bring about a group identity centered in worship of the God who made himself known in Christ. These have been sessions of sharing, singing, and prayer, with the remembrance of the death of Christ carrying a distinct secondary role. Other meetings have dealt primarily with discussions about the group. A limited number of individual concerns have been discussed whenever members chose to raise them.

Membership has not been clearly defined at any time. Since there was no established group or members with previous experience, there was a hesitance to pass judgment on others in the determination of membership. Instead, there has been an attempt to express a common base of understanding and a basic willingness to participate in the statement of commitment. Voluntary acceptance of this statement through the attendance of the communion service planned for this purpose constituted membership. Participation in other meetings has not been determined by membership. During the first year several people participated in all aspects of the church without taking the step of commitment. As yet, there has been little experience with accepting new members after the initial formation of the fellowship. Such action would likely be seen as dissolving the existing relationship between members and setting up a new one encompassing as well those who wish to enter.

Other activities of the church are scheduled or formally sponsored by the whole group. The expression of the church is through the efforts of the individuals with a limited amount of smaller group action. There has been a conscious attempt to be aware of people and to meaningfully relate to individuals as persons.

The existence of the Christian fellowship is seen as an honest struggle to be obedient to the will of God here and now. There has been no attempt to compete with or stand in opposition to local congregations or other Christian activities. Membership did not imply breaking existing church relationships. Participation in local church services, the Student Christian Association, and other service opportunities has been encouraged.

Lessons We Have Learned

In the face of many difficulties the participants in a church may well become discouraged in any one year. Even if failure should come, the experience attained would make the effort worthwhile. To define a church as people rather than a program or structure is so foreign to our way of thinking that any experience that young people obtain will prepare them to better participate in such ventures as they meet them again in our rapidly urbanizing society. Some of the experience gained to this point is summarized as follows:

1. One of the functions of a church is to be a redemptive community. Our church has not really served in this capacity. One of the reasons for this failure is the mistrust that still prevails between members. It takes time to learn to know each other and to overcome the negative attitudes toward each other which have developed on other contacts. Our fellowship is still too easily diverted by differing viewpoints which draws attention away from our central concern of being obedient to God.

2. The decision to hold unstructured meetings has served a useful purpose in that weekly meetings have not separated worship from the rest of life. Nevertheless, would individuals entering our meetings know God is present? How does a group move beyond existing knowledge to new frontiers? Will class work do this? Possibly the best approach is for study to take place outside of the group meetings, but this must be consciously recognized if there is to be continuous growth in understanding.

3. The idea of mission tends to conflict with establishing trust in each other so that sharing of ideas, concerns, and problems will take place. The acceptance of new members tends to disrupt existing relationships. A possible solution may be to work in smaller groups rather than attempting to keep all together in one meeting.

4. The church has not really served to help members decide the basic questions they face in life. As of now the church is only one of many activities in our lives and, therefore, not really in a position to know the implications of any one decision that an individual is facing. Likely the first decision to be made within the church is the participation in extra-curricular activities. Only after the members give the group this prerogative will there be the member involvement and program flexibility for effective action. The choice of extracurricular activities will then be made on the basis of what will best serve God's redemptive purpose in any given school year. This decision should be made at the end of one school year for

the coming year. After the church plays such a vital role for each member then it may also serve to help each to decide his major, life's partner, vocation, and place of service. Members would then go forth commissioned by the Christian Fellowship at Bluffton to serve in other areas of need.

5. The inability to make decisions in the face of distinctly diverse viewpoints has been a real problem. Group consensus is desirable to assure wholehearted participation in all aspects of the church, but the art of compromise must be developed. Things move fast on a college campus. The impatience that a stalemate generates readily tends to destroy the momentum of an idea. A possible solution without setting up an actual leadership might be the selection of a steering committee which continuously analyzes group meetings and makes recommendations when necessary. Then, should a meeting end in unresolved conflict, such a committee could present one or more compromise possibilities to be considered at successive meetings.

6. A college campus is a good setting for experimentation with new church structures. Students tend to be open to new ideas. Also, most are without family responsibilities so that there is flexibility for meeting and no need to provide services for children. At the same time, a church made up solely of students can present problems. Enthusiasm runs high when everything is going well, but a structure as complex and demanding as a church is likely to face numerous and difficult problems. In a college setting it is somewhat unpopular for one to give his life for a cause. To make a church work effectively, members must give their life, especially when difficulties arise.

8

Christian Communal Living on the Tabor Campus

STEVE BEHRENDS

At the beginning of the 1965–66 school year four of us decided to try an experiment in Christian communal living. After receiving the administration's permission, we set up housekeeping in a large two-story house. We pooled all of our money, filled the cupboards with canned food, and prepared ourselves for a traumatic experience. There was some reaction among friends. Most of the reactions tended to be pessimistic. To most people the financial situation was the thing under trial, but this is only one small fraction of it.

We set out on this venture for several reasons. None of us lived in the dorm and felt the necessity for a dorm experience. We also wondered if the church structure as found in the New Testament was something feasible for this modern age. We wanted to develop a real openness and fellowship among us, and above all to strengthen our Christian lives, and to become, in every sense of the word, our "brother's keeper."

Although we were ready for a great experience, we didn't get the jolt we expected. We became to some degree open with each other, but not nearly as honest as we had hoped to be. Rather than tell our "brother" about some trait of his that needed correction or that was causing conflict, we would joke about it. We had become good friends. A few weeks before Christmas we had a breakthrough. One of the other three found the freedom to tell one some of the things he had against me. Since then things have been going fairly well. We have been able to break down some of the prejudices among us. I used to feel inferior to one of the other boys because he is a deep thinker, only to find out that he felt inferior to me because I was a chemistry major. We have found some real freedom, but not nearly as much as we had hoped for.

There have been and are many problems—personality conflicts and conflicts resulting from living and working this close together. We haven't used this experience to the fullest. The past several weeks we have been at a low point, reaching the bottom when we felt we couldn't talk to each other. This drop, as well as the other times of non-communication, was the result of not sitting down for a time of fellowship. We had been hurrying here and there, seeing each other only at mealtime. Now we are trying to sit down every other day for a time of devotions and fellowship. Our lack of discipline is the main reason why we have not received the full benefit of this project. We all realize now how much work it takes to develop a relationship on this level, and have had to recommit ourselves. I am hopeful that our relationships can deepen.

This experience has meant many things to me. Before last summer I had never really been open with anybody. I had always tried to solve my own problems. Last summer I developed an honest relationship with two people. This was a good background for this experience. This year I have been able to take a good look at myself and my motives for doing things. I have found out that I am not the good guy I used to think I was. The others have been quite instrumental in helping me to see myself.

As for my Christian life, it hasn't been strengthened the way I had hoped it would be. I was expecting to be having my devotions more regularly, and so on, but I hardly have any devotions at all due to my lack of discipline. I think it has been strengthened, though, in that God has become closer to me. In relating to other people, I have found it easier to become honest with them. This experience has had quite an effect on me. I do feel that it is practical.

9

Tabor College Christian Fellowship Association

For several months, Tabor students have been discussing among themselves the idea of the small-group fellowship. At a recent discussion at a Christian Fellowship Association meeting, students talked about the shortcomings of present "Christian activities" on campus. Students felt that our traditional large-group meetings, although sincerely planned to be of spiritual help, were not meeting the needs. Students came away from them unchanged, unaffected. It was just a time filler and if there was anything Tabor students don't need, it was something to simply take up another hour of their time.

What then would be meaningful? There was an overwhelming group consensus that there was a need for students to take off their masks and honestly share with one another. In the fellowship of a small group, students could seek God together and help each other in problems of Christian growth.

And so the Christian Fellowship Association decided to provide a flexible structure for setting up small groups. Sharing groups of a permanent nature with no more than six members have been set up. Membership in the group was determined on a free choice sign-up basis. The groups will meet weekly (and more often if they desire). They will follow the biblical guidelines of church fellowship: burden-bearing, prayer, searching the Scripture, service, and bringing others in. Some groups may be oriented to one area more heavily than another, but it is hoped that all these elements will be present. Those who have spent time in prayer and planning this venture have expressed the following hopes and ideals:

It is hoped that our concern and prayer for one another will not occur only at the time of our meeting together, but that we will think of each other often. In other words, membership in a group involves real commitment and responsibility to our fellow members. It is hoped that the small-group approach does not tend to divide Christians on campus into cliques, but that open communication between groups and between group members and students not formally members of our sharing groups will exist.

It is hoped that our burden-bearing and problem-sharing will not stay at the level of directionless group therapy sessions, but that our sharing will be for the purpose of helping each other. We can also share our joys and new insights and thus enrich each other's experiences.

Our approach to the study of the Scriptures together must not be to find something to support preconceived notions. We must approach the Word with willing, open minds.

Neither must we fall into the trap of rising no higher than a lot of intellectual discussion and debate, "talking about God rather than to him." In our groups we must not just talk about the Christian imperative, but follow it. We feel this should result in service.

The groups should also have a natural and sincere evangelistic thrust. An enthusiastic member of a group can say to his friends, "Come along tonight and listen. See what you think of the whole idea." Others should be invited to observe and encouraged to join the group if they would like to. This is one reason the groups are small in members to begin with. They are designed for growth. When one group grows too large for open, balanced communication, it should be willing to divide in two.

The non-Christian or the discouraged Christian on our campus is often calloused to "too much religion." He will respond only to something that is sincere, worthwhile, and meaningful. Our groups can be just this.

Is this all too idealistic, too optimistic? Perhaps. We have discussed what we might do if certain problems arise. And yet we are optimistic. Perhaps we are optimistic because we can see already on campus, active, vital sharing groups, organized independently, which report that they have benefited from their mutual involvement.

The success of this "venture" certainly will not be judged by numbers. Naturally, initial sign-ups are expected to be small, for joining a group is a sign of concrete commitment. Anyone signing up should be thoroughly aware of what he is doing, of the responsibility that becomes his when he joins. Success, if judged at all, will be judged only in the individual lives of the participating members.

We definitely felt that God has led in beginning these sharing groups. But we must be honest and admit that we do not know what the outcome will be. That we must leave in God's hands.

Perhaps through this leap of faith we can together grasp the meaning of true discipleship. Then the possibilities are limitless and exciting.

10

The Church on Eastern Mennonite College Campus

Glenn M. Lehman

Our's is an age, as Albert Einstein once said, of perfect means and confused goals. Could this apply to the YPCA of EMC? Is our generation, which is now inhabiting the "ivy halls," fulfilling to any higher degree the purpose of being the church on campus than did their predecessors fifty years ago? Can we with our more perfect means say we are a more biblical church than those who have gone before? To this our posterity will have to give the answer. We cannot.

In this paper I hope to raise for discussion several general problems a Christian college faces in understanding itself as a church and several specific problems EMC and its Student Church faces.

Student Church is new at EMC. It has just passed its second birthday. Student Church is the largest body of students who worship together. Other bodies meet at our Y churches or at the Park View Church. About 175 students attend Student Church each Sunday at 10:00 AM. The service consists of Bible reading, prayer, a sermon by the student pastor or another faculty member or visitor, monetary giving for expenses and for other needs, such as Mennonite Broadcasts, or relief in Vietnam, or

Voluntary Service in some large city. Also part of the worship is led by an octet. Sometimes we have several minutes of silent meditation.

After the corporate worship period, at 11:00, the students (at least sixty of them) move into a smaller study or sharing group. One of these groups is what we call Missionary Fellowship, another group studies the Sunday-school lesson, another group is engaging in Acts Alive, still another group may discuss the sermon.

Student Church is led by three students appointed by the YPCA and the student pastor and the dean of students. These five persons are called the Student Church Council and they are immediately responsible to plan each service and to forge the larger Student Church operating philosophy.

Other students, in groups of eight to twenty, worship at what are called Y churches. They are actually small Virginia Conference "missions," five of which are in towns and five of which are rural. Most of the students serve actively in the local program as song leaders or Sunday-school teachers. These groups meet once during the week to fellowship and pray for their respective churches. The YPCA tries to keep a feeling of spiritual kinship between the Student Church goers and the Y Church goers.

A significant function of the church is that of loving the Lord Jesus Christ with all our being. This very definitely has personal meanings, but does it not also involve our corporate worship program? John Stott in his timely book, *Basic Christianity*, says that God offers three solutions to man's threefold problem. Man's alienation from God was redeemed by the death of Jesus Christ; his bondage to self has been freed by the Holy Spirit, who makes regeneration and the resultant new nature and freedom from bondage possible; and finally a worldwide brotherhood, the Christian church, in which people are bound together by love, resolves men's conflict with the rest of mankind. This unique purpose for the formation of the church must be realized in its various programs, for indeed this ideal need be the real pulse of the corporate worship.

One of the significant functions of being the church is being a redemptive fellowship. But basically it involves a group within which all the dynamic aspects of group relations take place. Christ's mention of this is very clear in Matt 22:36–39, when He says that the second great commandment is loving our neighbor as ourselves.

Yet another function of the church on campus must definitely involve a means of mission. Whatever form this may take, it must necessarily be felt if the church is to be pronounced healthy, for the church without a mission is a church without a future. We might ask if a campus church can have a mission, and if so, what is it?

We should relate this more clearly to our situation. If we use mission as a label for everything, a twilight hue confuses or obscures our goals. Have we at EMC caught the spirit of what it is to be a servant to mankind or a witness among many? Have we a mission as a corporate body of believers? Each Sunday we make our pilgrimage to our little Meccas out in the countryside where we offer our libations, leading a few songs or teaching a nursery Sunday-school class, only to return on furlough for the following six days. Does a college student have a mission or is theoretical concern enough since his service will come after his four years of training? There must be a mission for him during his college experience because Christ made no exception in Matthew 24 for any Christian to spend a few years on leave.

Is the student who remains on campus for his worship experience none of the elect? And can he experience church apart from mission? We should never be so limited in our thinking that we cannot conceive of a mission in any situation. Student Church, to a certain degree, achieves the above prerequisites for church. In comparison to the former practice of meeting with the Park View congregation, Student Church is ably providing a more meaningful sense of belonging to and involvement in the group. Students generally are committed to this church and view it as "their" church, where they can express themselves rather than be there as observers only.

Student Church is providing students with a meaningful corporate worship experience. Several have expressed the opinion that it is easy to worship at Student Church. On the other hand, Student Church has not yet fully realized the meaning of what it means to be a redemptive fellowship and she has only partially realized what it means to be directly involved in missions. This is something more than giving our tithes and offerings for some mission program, for it must also relate us directly with people.

In conclusion, we could say that the church on EMC campus is attempting to exist as a part of the YPCA organizational structure and is struggling to find its goals and mission. We are not sure whether the persons who go to our Y churches are a part of our church or not. And in the future we see ourselves as moving in the direction of becoming one church body on campus with its mission both off and on the campus.

11

The Church on Campus, Present and Future

What Are the Issues?

Harold E. Bauman

The relation of church and campus has two aspects which are closely related: one, church and campus as faith relating to the task of education, and two, church and campus as organized religion relating to the persons involved in the campus. The first involves the famous question: What does Jerusalem have to do with Athens? While the second may include this aspect but more often refers only to helping the person on campus be Christian in their "spiritual life" and conduct. It does not relate faith or organized religion to the task of education.

History does not offer a ready solution for holding these two pairs of aspects together. Arnold Nash claims that the Colonial colleges were Christian only sociologically; the teaching was dominated by a-Christian assumptions. Required chapel and Sunday church attendance, required courses in doctrine and religion, high moral standards set by the colleges, and the presence of a Christian faculty characterized the colleges. But the Christian faith was not integrated with the teaching.

During the Jeffersonian period this same situation was duplicated in the establishment of many church colleges. However, in some of the earlier colleges and in some newly established ones, both the curriculum and the administration broke loose from any Christian moorings. During the last part of the nineteenth century and the early twentieth century, the state university emerged more predominantly. A trend toward the exclusion of theology and religion from the curriculum developed. Many church colleges were swept along in its path.

While this trend has reversed itself in the past two decades, the question of the relation of church and campus has moved to a fourth phase presently emerging which focuses upon the question: How can the church help students and faculty discover their Christian vocation as participants in the sphere of secular scholarship itself? Nash, as well as Moberly, calls for lay theologians in the campus community.

Another characterization of the relation of church and campus is given by Harvey Cox. The church first established its own colleges and universities as its way of dealing with higher education. When the institutions moved out of its control, the church worked through nearby residential congregations to render a special ministry to people involved in academic life. Cox says this method failed because functional relationships are more important than geographical communities. The third stage found the church trying to follow its students with the denominational student center as the "home away from home." This approach also fails because it makes the church an island unrelated to the academic community.

While we are still in stage three, there are encouraging signs which point to a new relationship of church and campus. Ecumenical teams of campus ministers, writes Cox, are developing which seek to serve the campus through study groups, personal contacts, and worship. Disciplined communities of students and faculty seek to engage the academic community on its own terms.

These two historical characterizations point up interesting parallels between the relationships of faith and education and the church and campus. One observation is that both relationships are now focusing upon the whole person as a Christian in interaction with the campus as education. The experience of "church" and "Christian" cannot be separated nor can the experience of "scholar" and "person." Attempts to find relationships between church and campus must involve all four dimensions.

This essay will attempt to define the issues in the relation of church and campus. A discussion of the issues involved in regard to the method to be used in seeking solutions will be followed by a discussion of the issues involved in the substance of the question itself. In the process some tentative directions will be indicated in the hope of arousing discussion contributing toward solutions.

The first issue in finding a method to solve the question of the relation of church and campus is in regard to the place of the New Testament. Does it prescribe the forms of the church for all time, or does it provide only the basic understandings of what it means to be church, which are then worked out in various forms throughout the ages? The changing forms of the church even in the New Testament period speak to the question. However, common in all such forms is the essence of the church, its tasks, and the kind of relationships within it.

A second issue in regard to method has to do with the place social sciences have in determining the forms of the church and their relationships to the campus. One cannot say that the forms are only a matter of opinion or personal preference unrelated to the task and essence of the church. Social sciences can contribute to understandings of group interaction and formations, but these are not determinative when it comes to the form of the church.

While some may hold that a given historical form of the church will fit all situations, one need only to ask, Which historical form? On the other hand, one is not left without any guides to test the expression of the church. The New Testament understandings of the essence and tasks of the church provided criteria for testing any new forms which may emerge. The forms of the church in any given situation are not to be anticipated but are found only inductively by walking in faithful obedience to these New Testament understandings.

What are the basic areas, then, in which issues will likely emerge in the actual relationship of church and campus? The most basic issue is, What is "church"? Church is often viewed as people participating in religious activities as individuals: hearing the Word preached and receiving the sacraments. Others see church primarily as correct religious structures: duly chosen officers, members rightly received, organizations, and meetings. Still others see the church as a select group of members with a leader who nurtures them in cultic in-group activities: church is privatized religion. The Anabaptist view roots the church in a commitment resulting in persons with changed lives who are bound together and who share certain relationships and tasks.

Specifically, to be church is to confess voluntarily Jesus as Lord and to worship Him; to be bound by the Holy Spirit into a new community which forgives, nurtures, admonishes, and supports; to enter into group decision-making on the consequences of the lordship of Christ in daily walk and relationships; and to enter into a servant ministry to the context where the church finds itself. The forms of church must be those which will facilitate the expression of these relationships and functions. The church on the campus, then, is those persons who have covenanted together in such a confession and to such purposes.

A second issue deals with how the church relates to the campus. While the corporate church (a given denomination) may make institutional provisions for higher education, including certain required religious courses and activities, this is not the church on the campus for Christian students and faculty. The corporate church may legitimately express interest in the Christians on campus by providing a pastor to work with them. Often such an approach has not resulted in a church experience with integrity, but rather in certain student organizations which are sponsors of various religious activities. Church for students is often participation in one or more such activities and/or attendance at the "worship service" of some residence congregation located on or near the campus.

According to the Anabaptist view of the church given above, the church on campus is those Christians (students and faculty) who covenant together to work out the meaning of worship, reconciliation, mutual growth, decision-making in response to the confession of Christ's lordship, and a servant ministry in their situation, in this case, as scholars in an academic community. Such a church will have within it many gifts; the pastoral leadership gift may be provided by the corporate church, not to provide program or activities on campus, but to assist the Christians on campus to be the church "at *academe*."

The third issue in the relation of church and campus is already suggested by the essential areas of being church: What is the mission of the church on campus? The task of scholarship is to pursue knowledge as far as it can, but it always ends with some questions unanswered. While the Christian does not use God to explain what he does not know, he does confess the ultimate mystery of knowledge. He acknowledges the sovereignty and "otherness" of God in worship. Does the academic pursuit stimulate more need for worship than do other vocations? What should be the nature of such worship on the campus? Tentative conclusions would indicate such worship should be related to the congregation of believers on campus and that the more frequent such worship services are held during the week, the less the need for worship on Sunday will be felt. The church on campus will arrange for opportunities for corporate worship for those who desire it.

The church on the campus is also a community of reconciliation: providing opportunities for self-discovery, healing broken relationships, and establishing bonds of support and encouragement to keep integrity in each believer's commitment. Guidance and support are offered to those facing particular decisions and crises: self-identity, vocational choice, marital choice, illness, and grief situations. Some aspects of these ministries are offered by the members of the church with special counseling arranged only when such skills are needed.

The confession of Christ as Lord of one's life and of the church leads the congregation to seek corporately the consequences of such a confession in the whole of life: character, interpersonal relationships, vocation, and the needs of society. The covenanted group seeks to be informed in biblical thought and in the human situation by whatever studies are necessary, wrestling with both components under the guidance of the Holy Spirit to a group consensus.

The meaning of Christ's lordship in the life of the scholar becomes one of the primary concerns of the church on campus. The gathered congregation seeks to equip each believer with an understanding of the Christian faith and to seek together the relation of such faith to the disciplines of the academic community. The church enters into conversation and search with the academic community on its terms to investigate the ultimate meanings which lie behind each discipline and its ways of knowing. This open examination of the truly secular can contribute to the church's understanding both of itself and of the human scene and aid the church in gaining clarification in regard to its own decisions on its servant ministry.

Such ministry is expressed not only in relating faith to disciplines but also in concern and compassion for individuals who are searching for wholeness in life. The servant ministry is also expressed in concern for the brokenness of society. At times the church may stand with other scholars in witnessing in the ills of society; at other times the church may need to stand alone. Concerns off-campus should not blind the church to its primary task of engaging the academic community in dialogue on the meaning of its framework and assumptions in its work of scholarship.

Such a range of essential tasks in being church raises the fourth issue in relating church and campus: What should be the form of the church on campus? The residential congregation serving persons in a geographical community has been the generally accepted pattern of church. Does the campus with its specialized function and the large gathering of persons participating in it call for the church on campus to become its own geographical community or shift the basis for the congregation to its functional community? The basis should be that which allows for equipping the believers for their specific tasks and facilitates decision-making and servant ministry in their context. These same criteria apply to the forms of the church also. All those who confess Christ as Lord and enter into the covenant of the church are welcomed as members. Activities of the academic community which do not have Christian commitment as their basis should be sponsored by student organizations which do not have Christian commitment as their basis for membership.

The fifth issue raises the question as to the locus of responsibility for the church on the campus. The guiding principle involved is that the Christian should be a responsible member in all the functions of the church where he participates. The responsibility for the life and form of the church lies with the believers involved, in this case, the Christian students and faculty. Does the problem of the rapid change of membership on the campus mean that the responsibility for church on campus devolves upon others? Does it mean the academic institution arranges with a residence congregation to provide worship services for the Christians who desire to attend them? How does such an arrangement meet the qualifications of being church?

Participation in church must come from a voluntary commitment. Once made, there is a shared responsibility to enable one another to fulfill this commitment. This is the meaning of being church. To remove this responsibility and its expressions from the Christians involved is to end with a pseudo church. This means that requirements in regard to religious practices by the academic administration is foreign to this view of the church.

One additional consideration has to do with the degree of maturity the student possesses and the kind of feelings and attitudes he expresses in regard to the church. Some students are more ready for responsible participation than others. The presence of faculty members in the congregation helps toward not only continuity but also a wider range of counsel and experience. The inclusion of the Christian student as a full participant in the life of the congregation may achieve growth toward his maturity more quickly than the withholding of responsibility.

A further consideration in the life of the church on campus is the assimilation of a large number of new members annually within a brief scope of time. The new students come with many ideas on what church is. Those upper-class students and faculty who worked through to a viable understanding of what it means to be church will need patience and understanding to help new students through a process which they themselves have already walked. What may seem to some an unnecessary experience of reopening some questions each fall will undoubtedly be a part of the experience of the church on campus. One might reasonably predict some changing forms so that the church on campus will always be somewhat experimental.

The search for the viable form of the church on campus must take into account the search for the renewal of the church throughout the world. Central to the whole venture is the understanding of what it means to be church. Emerging from the renewal efforts are emphases very similar to the understandings of the meanings of church used in this essay. What unique aspects may emerge on the campus are hardly predictable. When each member of the academic community who desires to walk in commitment to Jesus Christ is taken seriously, not as a transient or temporary or partly responsible member but on full terms with any other member of the congregation where he participates, and when the functional context and tasks of each member are taken seriously, then the church on the campus can come into its full realization.

Afterword

Virgil Vogt

The papers in this issue of *Concern* give some indication as to how and where the reality of the church as "church" is coming alive in the experience of persons on Mennonite college campuses. It is obvious that in spite of considerable variation in the extent and depth of the changes which are underway on these several campuses, many of these separate developments are moving along somewhat similar lines. The most thorough expression of this new direction (both in theory and in practice) has been found thus far at Bethel College, Newton, Kansas, where Albert Meyer served as dean and Walter Klaassen as professor of Bible.

The Meyer-Klaassen paper, which first appeared in July, 1964, was about twice its present length in the original mimeographed form. It included an extensive historical analysis of the sixteenth-century Reformation, seeking to clarify the unique contribution of the radical Anabaptist reformers. We have deleted this part of the manuscript on the assumption that most *Concern* readers are somewhat familiar with the emerging Anabaptist witness. It is worth mentioning here, however, to indicate that the present trend of these new campus efforts is being guided in part by an appreciation for the insights and experiences of the sixteenth-century Anabaptists.

To the extent to which the experience at Bethel (and the other campuses) does represent an openness to the concerns of the radical Reformation, it has significance far beyond the campus. It stands as a kind of preliminary sample for a fundamental restructuring which is urgently needed in many congregations, conferences, and church agencies. Here, too, we will find many points at which existing church patterns represent a denial of the "believer's church" vision which Mennonites officially espouse. This is not surprising when we realize that the basic style of congregational and conference life was clearly established in its present form before the "Recovery of the Anabaptist Vision" had emerged as a significant factor. The integrity of membership decisions, the practice of sharing and of binding and loosing, are all matters which need the same vigorous rethinking in any other church situations.

The problems that we face, however, may be more complex than we understand. In several of the papers we hear of "fringe" members. We learn of internal conflicts, of reluctance to be honest, of failure to carry discussion through to decision, of fearing to share and love and to bind and loose. And all of this has happened, not because of structural problems, but precisely within groups that have been structured so as to facilitate the process. These are indications that there is a part of the problem which needs to be more adequately dealt with in the theory and experience of these campus groups: the resistance within each of us to radical Christian obedience.

This problem stands somewhat in the background of most of these reports, although in several groups (as, for example, Bluffton and Tabor) they seem to have confronted this part of the problem more directly. We are tempted, I think, to overlook this side of it and to assume that if we can set up appropriate structures, people from our existing churches will get into them and will function together as Christians should. There is enough in these reports, however, to indicate that this is a shaky assumption. A lukewarm and compromising approach to Christianity has become too deeply ingrained in the very structure of our personalities. This too must undergo radical change. But how? Perhaps those who have some experience and theory about this part of the task can share it with us in another issue of *Concern*.

www.ingramcontent.com/pod-product-compliance
Lightning Source LLC
Chambersburg PA
CBHW022120160426
43197CB00009B/1093